In 1140, forty years after the death of Ruy Díaz de Vivar, an unknown poet in the Spanish kingdom of Castile wrote an epic account *Poema de Cid* of his national hero.

Chief Marshal of the royal army of King Sancho ll, Ruy Díaz, fell from favour when Sancho's brother came to the throne. Banished to the south, where Moorish invaders held sway, he fought as a mercenary both for the Moors and against them. But in 1094 he made his greatest mark on history by capturing the stronghold of Valencia. It was the beginning of the end of the Moorish occupation.

A single copy of the poem, with several pages missing, was all that survived for centuries, although other medieval poets were adding meanwhile to the legend of 'El Cid'. His renown grew and so did the stories attaching to his life, much as Robin Hood or William Tell gathered around them extravagant glories. To Spanish children today, the whole story of El Cid, from his banishment to his last legendary ride, is an accepted and well-loved part of their nation's history.

In modern times, the grandeur of the character has inspired further literature – such as Corneille's drama, *Le Cid*. This retelling owes a debt to all versions, written and spoken, of the Song of the Cid.

EL CID

Geraldine McCaughrean
Illustrated by Victor G Ambrus

Oxford University Press
Oxford New York Toronto

A Shameful Thing

Such a host of candles blazed along the King's table that they began to soften in their own heat and bend drunkenly this way and that. The wax made white pools and whorls among the silver dishes. It fell on to the long hair of noblemen slumped across their food, asleep.

The King himself had had rather too much wine. He went to lean an elbow on the table and slipped off it so that he slid sideways in his chair. It made him angry that Don Rodrigo Díaz de Vivar saw him slip.

'What's the matter with you, Don Rodrigo? Don't you care for the taste of Our wine?'

Halfway along the table, a tall, gaunt-featured man with a severe, immaculate beard sat erect on his hard, oak chair, his straight back touching the seat back without leaning against it. The skin around his eyes was so creased by the bright Spanish sun that he seemed to be peering penetratingly at those around him. His second cup of wine stood untouched beside his clean, abstemious trencher. The swell of his chest fell away to hardly any stomach at all. 'Like a crow,' said the King without meaning to.

'I beg your pardon, my liege?' said Don Rodrigo Díaz de Vivar.

'We said, you peck at your food like a crow,' said the King.

Just then, the Princes Diego and Fernando seized each other by the throat and rolled under the table with a crash. Everyone's attention was immediately on the noise of the brawl between their feet. The noblemen at the feast bleared down past their swelling stomachs into the darkness under the table. Bowls clattered and spilled on the benchtop. The melting candles jostled and swooned. A dish of olives overturned into the King's lap.

Count Ordoñez, probably the only other man still sober, thrust his head between his knees and hissed at his nephews, 'Stop that! Infantes, are you mad? The King will have you flogged! You'll be the ruin of our family.'

Chastened, the young Infantes crawled out from under the table and set off towards the door on their hands and knees, in the hope that the King would not see them go. It was a vain hope. The King was getting redder and redder in the face with a deadly mixture of drink and outrage. The boys' uncle had to distract his attention or risk a slur on his family name. He searched about for a way to do it, then said loudly, 'The poor little lads were overcome, I expect. There is a very strong smell of *peasant* in this room, wouldn't you say, Díaz of Vivar?'

There was a great sucking of teeth and glancing at the King, as the other nobles registered the insult and wondered what would come of it. Don Rodrigo Díaz did not stir except to peel an orange and hold each slice up to the light of the candles, looking for the pip. 'What can you mean, Count Ordoñez?'

'Just that there's no mistaking an upstart yokel. He smells different, whether or not his father was knighted in battle.'

The King picked his teeth intently, but his eyes gleamed with joy when he saw Don Rodrigo's elbow slip off the arm of his chair with astonishment.

'Surely you are not suggesting, Count Ordoñez, that the old, dead King was wrong to knight my father for the services done him?' said Don Rodrigo, with studied calm.

The King scowled. It was a good argument. How would Count Ordoñez disagree without saying something treacherous?

'Father? Oh then, you do call the man your *father*, do you? I heard tell that your mother couldn't get to the church in time before you were born.'

Howls of protest and roars of laughter disturbed all the dogs sleeping by the fire, and they raced around the room, barking.

King Alfonso knew that he should put a stop to Ordoñez' outrageous insults, but he was a little too drunk to find the words. . . . And besides, he was spellbound watching Don Rodrigo's knuckles whiten on the arm of his chair.

'Pray be more plain, dear Count,' said Don Rodrigo, although the trembling of his voice belied the seeming calm. 'What *can* you be implying?'

The Count was committed: too late to apologize. He had overstepped the mark of common courtesy. But his one eye on the King told him that he was safe. He leaned across the table and thrust his podgy face close up against those handsome, sunburned features he despised so much. 'I'm saying you're a bastard, Rodrigo Díaz. That's what I'm saying.'

'Ah. I see.' The reply was crisp and businesslike. His reflexes were not impaired by drink. His right hand flew up off the arm of the chair, took hold of the Count's beard, and tugged it down into the cup of wine.

That was all. Nothing else. All he did was to pull the Count's beard.

But the insult resounded off the mountains, blew the ash off a thousand noble hearths, and echoed through the family vaults of Castile so loudly that the dead sat up with startled questions.

'Did you see that? Did you? Did you see what he did, my liege?' spluttered Count Ordoñez, his beard dripping redly on to his chest.

The King closed his gaping mouth but his eyes still bulged. 'We saw it.'

'The bastard pulled my beard! That peasant discomforted a man of noble stock! That farmer's son of a slut paid me the ultimate insult! Me! Count García Ordoñez!'

'We saw it.' The King stood up. Everyone at table who was not already on his feet struggled to do the same. 'We saw it, Count Ordoñez,' said the King, 'and We shudder for you. We grieve for your ancestors whose spirits have been affronted. Rodrigo Díaz de Vivar, you have greatly displeased Us!'

Standing up now, Don Rodrigo reminded King Alfonso of that one thing he had never been able to forgive – the fact that he stood head and shoulders taller than the King. Don Rodrigo spread his big hands beseechingly. 'Does the King's heart not feel any pity for my dead parents whose good names have been called into doubt?'

'No!' squeaked the King shrilly. 'We never want to see your face again. We never liked you! Take yourself out of God's country and never come back . . . on pain of death!'

Even the dogs paused in their barking at the sound of the gasps and consternation in the room.

'Don Rodrigo banished?'

'The good man of Vivar banished?'

'The Conqueror banished?'

'The best soldier in Castile banished?'

'For defending his saintly mother?' The dogs began unanimously to howl.

'Banished?' whispered Don Rodrigo.

'If you are not out of Holy Spain three days from midnight, We charge Our soldiers to cut you down. And on pain of death will any citizen of Castile help you to safety. It's in the blood. That's plain to see. Nobility is in the blood. You are no true knight, sir!'

At the door of the room, grinning all over their acned faces and making threatening gestures with their dinner knives, the two Princes, Diego and Fernando, stood barring Rodrigo's way. Rodrigo looked contemplatively down into the palm of his right hand, then used it to slap each boy soundly across the face. They went sprawling.

Tomorrow the King would regret the wine that had washed away all the elegant good manners from his court. He would see the looks of bewildered shock on the faces of his nobles. There would be murmurs about the quality of the King's justice. Already Alfonso began to eye the drunkards slumped across his table and wonder when the like of 'the Conqueror' would sit there again.

'We shall call him back and forgive him . . . shall We?' he said to his reflection in the mirror that night.

But his reflection said, 'Why should We? Did he plead for mercy? Did he apologize to the Count Ordoñez? No! And anyway – We never liked him, with his po-face and his moderate drinking and his prayers night and morning and his being taller than Us. Let him go.'

The King said, 'He might wreak some useful havoc if he's driven out into the land of the godless Moors. . . . He's such a good soldier.'

'Quite,' said his reflection.

The King nodded thoughtfully. 'Hmmm. But shall We be thought *unjust*, hereabouts?'

His reflection gave a snarl of a smile. 'We may be merciful to his pretty wife and family. They shall be permitted to stay on the family estate at Vivar. That's mercy enough for any beard-pulling peasant!'

Exiled

Along the walls of the white halls of Vivar, all the curved pegs were empty of coats and cloaks. Like the horns of furious bulls, the empty pegs curved out from the white walls of Vivar. Not one fleece-lined cloak remained; not one braided woollen coat. They swung instead from the shoulders of Vivar men, and the narrow streets clattered with the hooves of horses and mules. The air was full of dust, where the women shook out saddle blankets that had lain folded on shelves for years. The dust stung their eyes – or so they said, as they dried the tears with their sleeves.

High on the hill, in the monastery of Santa María, the bell in its thick, grey tower clanged with a single, dismal note, as if to say:

'The King has spoken!
The King has spoken!'

Don Rodrigo Díaz de Vivar embraced his lovely wife and dried her tears. 'South, then,' he said. 'Into the lands of the godless Moors and out of God's holy Castile and the light of your eyes and the eyes of my lovely daughters. But think. At night the same stars will look down on you and on me until we are together again.'

'But exile!' cried Doña Jimena, unable to accept his fate so calmly. 'Such a large punishment for such a small offence!'

Rodrigo laughed. '*I* was *greatly* offended! Otherwise I would never have pulled the Count Ordoñez' beard. It is just unfortunate that the gracious King took his side against me. No more. Heaven forbid I should speak treason or complain. I am the property of the King Alfonso to do with as he chooses. I must bear my sufferings like a man!'

But when the Abbot Don Sancho came down the hill from the

monastery, leading by the hand Rodrigo's little twin daughters, Rodrigo dropped his bridle and saddlebags and ran and hugged each girl close to his chest. 'Elvira! . . . Sol! . . . Your father has to go away. But you see what good hands I'm leaving you in? The Abbot here will be as good a father to you as ever I was. But you must help him by being good girls and taking great care of your mother. Help to keep her cheerful, and remember to say your prayers . . .'

'Yes, papa.'

'. . . and study your books . . .'

'Yes, papa.'

'. . . And if . . . And if, for any reason, I don't . . . come back to you . . . you will try to remember my face, won't you?'

'Not come back, papa?'

Doña Jimena came and took her daughters' hands and stood face to face with her husband. 'It is time for you to go, Don Rodrigo Díaz de Vivar. Your followers are waiting.'

The Don drew his sleeve across his eyes and nodded. He saddled his horse, Babieca, and drove his boots deep into the shining brass stirrups. 'You are right, lady. My prayers keep you company until I return home or send for you to join me. Who knows? Perhaps while I am gone, I can find two fitting husbands for these daughters of ours. What do you say, Don Sancho?'

The Abbot came and stood on the other side of Rodrigo's horse so that no one should see the money that passed between them. 'Here's all the money I have,' said the Don. 'Take care of them, whatever happens. I'll send more if I can.'

The round-faced monk gave a guffaw of laughter as he kissed the nobleman's hand respectfully. 'And what will you be doing to earn more money? Shearing sheep for the Moors? Farming corn and squash on some Moorish allotment? I know you better than that, Don Rodrigo. I know what kind of adventures lie ahead of you . . . In the meantime, how will you pay your men and keep them in food and leather if you have given all your wealth to me?'

'Ah, well . . .' Don Rodrigo looked quickly over each shoulder. 'I have a little scheme in mind. You see that leather trunk being tied to the grey mule?' And he leaned down to whisper in the monk's ear.

But the Abbot would have none of it. 'Don Rodrigo Díaz de Vivar, don't tell me your rascally plans. When the moon rises tomorrow, you must be out of Castile, on pain of death. Don't waste any more time on words,' said Don Sancho, blessing his friend with the sign of the cross. 'Go now. You're rich in friends, even if you're poor in gold: I don't fear for

you. But you really should put the great plains between you and the King's anger.'

Don Rodrigo nodded and, clicking his tongue to stir his horse to a trot, he dared neither a backward glance nor a wave of his hand as he rode out of Vivar, banished from his home for ever.

Burgos Town stood only a short way over the horizon, and there was not a man there but he knew Don Rodrigo who owned the estates of Vivar.

They knew his handsome, prancing horse; they knew his long, gaunt face with eyes screwed up against the glare of the yellow plain as a sailor's eyes crease against the brightness of the sea. They knew the straight line of his back beneath his cloak, and the tread of his boots when he came on foot.

But as he and his men rode into Burgos, every door was shut, every shutter closed. Dogs slept in the streets. Cats washed in the sun. But not a man or a woman was out of doors; not a face looked out of a window.

The dust from under his horse's hooves blew ahead of Rodrigo down the empty street, and settled against bare, baked mud and white-painted walls. Not a skirt swept the market square. Not a cart-wheel rolled over the lacy pattern of cart tracks on the main street. No voice broke the silence; only the dismal barking of an unseen dog and the crack of washed clothes flapping on a line.

'Ho, there! What's amiss!' called Don Rodrigo. But his voice fell and died, like a bird, in the narrow space between the houses. He turned to his closest, most trusted friend, 'Strange times, Alvar Fañez. Can a town die like a tree, overnight?'

Alvar Fañez spurred his little roan mare up and down, up and down the street, shouting up at the windows: 'Hoi! Open up! Who's there? Show some respect! Show some hospitality! Will no man bid farewell to the Don of Vivar and sell him a loaf of bread for the journey?'

Don Rodrigo called him back. 'To the miller's house. He'll give us provender. He's a friend of mine.'

But the miller's store was locked and bolted, and the shutters were closed as tight as eyes. Hearing a scuffle of movement indoors, Don Rodrigo lost patience and rode at the door, kicking at it with his spurred boot – *crash*, and again *crash*. The rowel fell from his spur like a falling star and suddenly, as if from nowhere, a little girl came and picked it up. She reached it up into Rodrigo's hand. She did not smile, and her eyes darted this way and that.

'Thank you, little maid. Tell me, are you all alone in this big town? Is there no one but you to give me a friendly greeting?'

The little girl wrung her apron in her two hands and when at last she spoke, the words babbled out of her like water from a fountain. 'The King sent word yesterday. No one's to speak to you or help you or give you shelter . . . not food nor drink nor straw . . . The King sent word. Anyone who opens his door to you will have his house taken away and his eyes dug out and his head cut off and his body buried away from the church, without a funeral! Mother says it's a shame for such a good man to have such a cruel master. Sorry, Don Rodrigo, sir. Sorry, sorry, sorry!' And she darted away, her bare feet lifting tufts of dust.

Don Rodrigo sat for a moment staring at the locked door. In that moment, he knew the sharpness of exile, knew that he was cut off from his home country as rind is cut off a cheese with wire, as meat is cut from the bone with a knife.

Then Babieca tossed her head, and the Don drove his heels into her flanks. 'Come, Alvar Fañez! Come, men! And praise God in your hearts for sending these hardships! Our souls will be all the stronger – like swords tempered in the fire!'

As the Don of Vivar galloped out of town, the windows and doors creaked open behind him, and a hundred unhappy heads leaned out to watch him go. 'Shame on the King Alfonso,' muttered the people of Burgos. 'A good man should have a better master.'

Since no one in Burgos dared shelter Rodrigo under his roof, he camped that night by the riverside and sent his men to scavenge after rabbits and fish for their supper. But it seemed a poor way to live out the rest of their lives. The faithful Alvar sat at a distance from his master and did not speak, knowing that the Don's heart was full of disgust and regret as well as thoughts of Doña Jimena and the little girls. The river slipped by noiselessly, like a lost opportunity.

Then the ground began to shake, and birds disturbed from the ground spiralled upwards to mingle with the circling bats. The kind of singing that spills out of taverns at midnight came rolling through the twilight and a huge wagon wallowed into sight with a bow-legged man standing up to shake the reins and encourage his two clumping horses. Behind the cart a string of armed men jangled and rattled along, joining in the chorus of the cart driver's song.

Alvar Fañez jumped up and drew his sword, thinking that the King had sent troops to speed the exile out of Castile. But Don Rodrigo spread his arms wide and greeted the cart driver with a crowing cheer: 'Martin! God bless you for a noisy cockerel! You'll wake the King in León with your singing! What brings you out of Burgos while the inns are open? Join us for supper if you've an appetite for air and water!'

The miller of Burgos jumped down. 'I had it more in mind to eat roast chicken and fresh bread myself. If I don't lighten this wagon of mine, it'll burst at the seams. There are supplies enough in here to take you and your men to the southern sea and back.'

'What, Martin? Haven't you seen the King's decree forbidding anyone to help me or cheer me or supply my needs?'

'Acch, you know me, Don Rodrigo, your honour. I never did learn to read. So he'll take my home? I won't be needing it, will I, if I'm to go adventuring with the Don of Vivar? So he'll dig out my eyes? Not if I see

him coming, he won't. So he'll cut off my head? It takes more than that to stop Martin the Miller singing! Oh, and these young men I've brought with me, they feel much the same about the good King and his royal decree. So here we are, and yonder's the pagan land full of godless Moors sitting in their golden castles. So make room round your camp fires, won't you? There's more men than you few from Vivar who want a taste of exile where the winters are warm!'

That night the camp fires laid a cheerful rind of gold on the quiet flowing river. Don Rodrigo lay down on the damp earth wrapped in his cloak and watched the comforting flicker through half-closed lids. Soon the gold gave way to the reflected silver of the moon. Then that too set. Only one day remained in which to leave Castile before the King's troops came howling after him to extinguish all his fires. Such a large punishment for pulling a beard. And such a small beard, too. Rodrigo fell into a strangely deep sleep, fringed with dreams as a Castilian castle wall is fringed with banners.

He dreamed that the angel Gabriel rose out of the river and stood beside him, the moonlight dripping off his unfurled wings. 'Hail, Don Rodrigo Díaz de Vivar. The treasure-house of the world grew richer on the day that you were born, and the planets danced. The King's anger is fierce, but your fist is fiercer. This journey of yours will make you greater and not less. So rise early and travel far. The angels of heaven fly in the wind-crack of your banner.' And it seemed that the angel reached out and seized Rodrigo by his beard and that his head was engulfed in fire.

When Rodrigo woke, the first rays of the sun were shining in his face. He rose to his knees and crossed himself, his fingers lingering on the tip of his beard. 'Before God I vow that no blade shall touch this beard until I have won glory for God and forgiveness from the King. On the heads of Sol and Elvira I vow it!' And he stood up, grinning at the prospect of the day ahead and the memory of his dream.

Changing Fortunes

'Who is it, brother Rachel?'

'Come and see, brother Vidas.'

'I can't spare the time, brother Rachel.'

'Then I won't waste my breath, brother Vidas.'

The man at the table sprinkled sand over the loan agreement he had just been writing, to dry the ink. The spare sand he tipped into a dish (to be used another time). Irritably he crossed to the window where his business partner was leaning out. 'Look at the light you're letting out, brother. Do you think candles cost nothing? Close the shutters.'

'But there's someone knocking. There are horses in the street. I can't make out who . . .'

'You know we never open the door after dark, brother Rachel.'

'It lets out the light, brother Vidas.'

'It lets in the robbers, brother Rachel.'

But the knocking continued, and Rachel and Vidas leaned farther and farther over the sill in trying to see who was down below. Suddenly the rider lit the tar-dipped torch in his fist, and it flared up just below their noses. Rachel and Vidas pulled in their heads like tortoises and slammed the shutters.

'It's him, brother Vidas!'

'It is, brother Rachel!'

'We mustn't speak to him . . . the King's decree!'

'No more eyes!'

'No more head!'

'*No more property!*' They clung to each other and, when the knocking started again, called out, 'Glory and honour are ours this day because you have deigned to visit us, Don Rodrigo Díaz de Vivar. *But do go away!* The King's decree, you know . . .'

'Ah, but I was in need of financial advice, good sirs.' (Rodrigo's deep voice filtered sonorously through the shutters.) 'So I thought at once of my good friends, Rachel and Vidas.'

The money-lenders looked at each other and blew out the candles. 'He hates us, brother Rachel. He always did.'

'Everybody hates us, brother Vidas. Everybody always has.'

From outside the window came the sound of a heavy load dropped from the back of a mule. 'It's about my treasure,' called Don Rodrigo loudly. 'I need somewhere to store it.'

Rachel and Vidas raced down the stairs, falling over the piles of useful objects they had squirreled away over the years in their tall, rock-hewn, one-windowed house. By the time the brothers opened the door, Martin

the Miller and Alvar Fañez stood at either end of an immense, wood-ribbed, brass-bound, leather trunk, their legs buckling under the weight of lifting it. Don Rodrigo walked indoors ahead of it, and allowed the money-lenders to kiss his hands respectfully.

'Mostly gold objects . . . some silver . . . and a certain amount of jewellery. In fact this trunk contains all the booty that I kept for myself after the siege of Zamora,' he said, plodding up the staircase while the cobwebs overhead caught light and shrivelled in the flames of his torch. 'But no actual money,' he said, turning at the doorway to stare penetratingly into the faces of Rachel and Vidas. 'Nothing I can use to feed and clothe the young men who have sacrificed so much to follow me into exile. I have hopes, of course . . . But in the meantime I must raise money the best way I can. So here's my proposition . . .'

While Don Rodrigo talked, Rachel and Vidas prowled round and round the trunk where Martin and Alvar had set it down. They fingered the wooden ribs, they stroked the brass binding, but a heavy padlock hung from the metal tongue of the lock.

'I wish to borrow six hundred marks for one year,' said Don Rodrigo brusquely. 'At the end of that year I shall send you your six hundred, plus two hundred in interest and another two hundred for the kindness you will do me in minding my treasure. Then you will send my trunk to me.'

'And what if your adventures don't bring you such fine sums of money?' said Vidas sharply.

'Then you may seize on the contents of the chest, of course. If I don't send word on the appointed day, or if I cannot send you one thousand marks, the chest is yours and all the treasure in it. Until then, the lid stays shut.'

Vidas scattered all the documents off his desk in his search for an unmarked roll of vellum. His pen scratched furiously. The ink stained his fingers red. He spattered hot wax recklessly across the foot of the contract. 'A bargain, Don Rodrigo Díaz! Fetch six hundred marks, brother Rachel.'

'Six hundred, brother Vidas?' wailed Rachel querulously.

'Six hundred, brother Rachel! Lift the slabs in the cellar and quickly!'

So Rachel lifted six of the slabs in the cellar of the tall, rock-hewn house, and fetched out the earthenware jars that were hidden beneath them, each of which contained a hundred marks.

When Don Rodrigo left, the moon was high and the hours were short which King Alfonso had allowed him to quit Castile. The money-lenders' marks hung heavy in the saddlebags of Alvar Fañez, and slowed their gallop towards the safety of exile.

'Safety?' said Vidas to his business partner. 'Rodrigo the Bastard safe in exile? He'll be chopped to messes by Moorish swords within the month and all his followers with him. It's certain death down there, and I like dealing with dead men! Let's see what treasure we've bought ourselves with a paltry six hundred. Fetch a poker, brother Rachel!'

'Right away, brother Vidas!'

It took hammer and poker and brute strength to force the lock on Rodrigo's treasure chest. Inside it they found a tree trunk, a dozen rocks and just enough of the dusty red soil from Vivar as would fill the six holes in their cellar floor.

'Six hundred marks, brother Vidas!'

'Six hundred marks, brother Rachel . . . for a box of dross. May the Moors spit him over their kitchen fires and spend all year in roasting him – Rodrigo the Bastard!'

'It was no lie,' said Don Rodrigo sombrely, though Alvar Fañez was still laughing. 'That trunk contained no less treasure than I kept for myself after the siege of Zamora.'

'Absolutely,' sniggered Alvar.

'Don't doubt it,' giggled Martin the Miller.

'I mean, to lie would be to sin,' said Don Rodrigo sternly, disapprovingly. He saw no humour in the situation, no humour at all.

His friends straightened their faces and nodded grimly. Then Alvar Fañez spluttered, and both he and Martin roared with laughter again.

They crossed out of Castile at midnight, between the teeth of a wild and snarling mountain range. In the very minute that King Alfonso's doom fell on the Master of Vivar, Don Rodrigo and a following of three hundred men topped a mountain and saw, laid out beneath them, a deep wooded valley in the moonlight. Far in the distance gleamed the walled city of Castejón.

'You see how this valley is held in the grip of night?' said Don Rodrigo. 'And yet in the morning, night will give it up to day without a sound or a struggle. That city down there is held just as tight in the black grip of the Moors. But tomorrow afternoon it will be in Christian hands, and with hardly the flash of a sword!'

At first light, the people of Castejón woke to a morning of mist. The guards ranged along the wall peered across a valley clogged with cloud and which seemed to crinkle as the sun drew up the dank fog of morning.

The gates were dragged open by black hands – as they had been dragged open for a century, ever since the Moors occupied Castejón Unsuspecting, the workers strolled or rode out to tend the crops in the

in the surrounding fields, to chop wood in the dark green forest, to feed the animals that flecked the open fields. Soon the fortress town was deserted, and no one thought to close the heavy gates or strain their eyes to make out the dark shapes moving among the trees. Deer, surely.

All at once, like a pack of timber wolves speeding to pull down a traveller, Don Rodrigo and one hundred of his armed men burst from the trees and galloped furiously across the open ground in front of Castejón, in at the open gates. Hooves skidded on cobbles and struck sparks. Blades hacked slivers of wood from the doorposts of houses, like cork oaks are flayed to make their sap trickle. Startled soldiers, set running by the noise, found themselves face to face with the foaming muzzles of charging horses, deafened by the rattle of snaffle, bridle, bit, and the the shouts of *'Castejón for God and Rodrigo Díaz!'*

The guard were out of armour – vulnerable in their soft woollen shirts, out of reach of their curved silver swords. Their dark eyes were ringed with the blue-white of terror, and their sandals skidded on the cobbles and spilled them under Babieca's hooves. They scrambled away, hugger-mugger, to the castle keep and once inside they shot the bolt – prisoners in their own city. Rodrigo circled the keep with his one hundred men and, from behind its massive walls of rock, Moorish cries of fright oozed through the arrow slits.

Out in the fields, one by one, the Moorish farmers working waist-deep in wheat, suddenly disappeared from sight, like paddlers pulled under the sea by an unexpected current. The shepherd going to fetch his stray animal from a thicket disappeared in a flurry of leaves. The goat-herd looked up from playing his pipe to see a Castilian sword at his throat. And the women doing their washing at the river bank saw reflections in the water of the faces of white men standing over them.

An hour or so later, Alvar Fañez brought home his captives to pen them with the others in the castle keep. 'You've done well, Master,' he said.

'And you've done better than well, old friend,' said Rodrigo Díaz. 'You shall have one fifth of all the booty we take from this city!'

Alvar curled his top lip proudly as he had often seen the Don of Vivar do, and he smoothed his hair. 'This was nothing. This was just goat-herding. I won't accept so much as a brass curtain hoop until I've done something truly *notable* in your service – something that will be spoken of at the court of King Alfonso and raise the eyebrows of my fair-weather friends there!'

So he and all Rodrigo's three hundred men handed in the things they found in the houses and took from their prisoners – horses and bracelets and lamps and coins and sheepskins and sweetmeats and gowns and works of art. They threw what they found on to the treasure-heap with a flick of the wrist and a shrug – as if wealth had never been to their taste; as if serving Rodrigo Díaz was their one and only joy.

He, of course, divided it into three hundred equal shares and gave it back to them as wages (keeping nothing for himself and nothing for the proud and loyal Alvar Fañez). *Then* he saw their eyes shine with a new depth of devotion – as the hounds in a kennel look with desperate love at the man who brings them meat. Rodrigo of Vivar would make them rich. That was why they had left behind their homes, families and good names and followed him into exile in the godless South.

'So, Don Rodrigo Díaz. You have found yourself a new home,' said Martin the Miller, running a critical eye over the dour stone houses of Castejón.

'There's no water,' said Rodrigo. He was up on the ramparts, thoughtfully staring out over the wall. 'And this place clings to Castile like a nettle caught in the hem of its cloak. My lord King Alfonso might not like me to lurk so close. And besides . . . no water inside the walls. How could a man withstand an enemy siege? . . . What city is that over there?'

The Castilians did not know, so they ran to fetch the Moorish ruler of the town from the keep prison. He was small – or seemed small, his chest hollowed, his shoulders slumped, his head sunk forward and rolling with misery. 'Does it begin with me, then? The killing?' he said through his heavy accent. 'Would that the killing could start and end with me, but you will chew us over, you Christians, until there is not a child left to cry.'

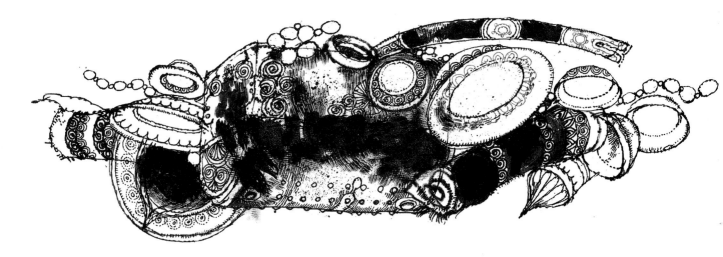

'What city is that in the distance?' said Don Rodrigo interrupting him.

'That? That is Hita. Will you slaughter my brothers there next?'

'What price do you suppose the good people of Hita would pay for this town and the people in it?' The Don appeared to be thinking out loud, but he did not miss the flash of hope which lit his prisoner's face. He went on: 'I don't much like this Castejón. It's not the place I want to live out my life. But why should perfectly good houses stand empty? Much better that your people should go on living in them as if nothing had ever happened – well, I a little richer and they a little poorer. So – if you would ride over there and suggest that they finance my journeying (that's to say, pay me to go away), I'll continue on my way and everyone will be happy.'

The Moor's happiness knew no limits. He knelt and kissed the Don's hand. 'Are you truly a Christian like that dog King Alfonso, sir, that you deal so graciously with your prisoners? Surely your religion cannot be that of the cruel and barbarous white men of the North? Surely you must have Muslim blood running in your . . .'

'Go,' said Don Rodrigo disapprovingly. And the Moor went, at the gallop, and negotiated a ransom of three thousand silver marks for Castejón and the freedom of all its citizens.

As the Don de Vivar took possession of the ransom and divided it equally between his three hundred followers, he sent word that the keep should be opened and that the Moorish prisoners should muster in the front-keep yard where he could address them.

'I free you that you may not think badly of me or my God! I do not want enemies at my back! I have it in mind to live out my days in a certain city not far from here: the city of Alcocer. If any warrior among you cared to join my army, he would of course share in the treasure to be won when that city falls into my hands!'

Murmured astonishment swept the yard like a breeze in a wheatfield. 'Black faces among white?' 'Moors and Christians together?'

Don Rodrigo waited for silence to fall again. 'Why not? No horse judges a rider by the colour of his skin: only by the strength of his knees and his use of the whip. The colour of your faces means nothing to me! I see only the spirit in a man's heart, the pith in his sword arm and the booty over his shoulder! Enough of your superstition! I say let us make an army that will be the scourge of all Spain!' (Although he breathed in an aside, 'Except for the realm of King Alfonso, may-his-glory-increase, of course.')

From that day onwards, the army of Don Rodrigo de Vivar was chequered as black and white as the marble courtyards of flowery Granada or the dapple on the ground beneath the leaves of a cork-oak tree.

The
Sieger
Besieged

The walled city of Alcocer was set on a bald, windy knoll, and no trees or tall maize corn grew to hide Rodrigo's approach. In any event, an army of six hundred men cannot be hidden, nor news of it kept secret. The inhabitants of Alcocer heard tell he was coming and shut the gates of the city. They could not be taken captive with one bold charge and an hour's patient trickery.

So Don Rodrigo set down tents on the grass below the walls, and day by week besieged the frightened city. Not a wagon of food could go in. Not a stone water jar could go out to be filled at the river. But though the sun scorched down day after day, and dried the sweat out of black and white skin, sieger and besieged alike, thirst did not drive the men and women of Alcocer to surrender. There had to be a well inside the walls. A man can brave hunger for a long, long time, but without water, he will sell his soul for a drink after a week.

'The godless King of Morocco is busy just now with his civil wars,' said Rodrigo in confidence to Alvar Fañez one night. 'But that won't save us for ever. We must capture this city or we must leave it alone before Morocco sends troops to beat us off.'

Alvar Fañez gnawed on a leg of chicken and watched his master throw pebbles thoughtfully at the toes of his boots. After a while he asked, 'And which shall we do, Don Rodrigo Díaz?'

Don Rodrigo looked up smiling and said, 'Both.'

The people of Alcocer looked over their battlements next morning, one
hand gripping their empty stomachs, one hand gripping a cup of water
from the well in the market place, and they said, 'Is there a mist?'

There was no mist.

'Is it hunger playing tricks with our eyes?'

But their eyes did not deceive them.

The Don's army had gone. The circles of a thousand dead camp fires
marked the ground like the scars of smallpox, but the Don's army had
gone. Only one embroidered tent, one flapping and mysteriously lonely
tent remained, like the tether for a goat after the goat has been devoured.

'The Christian dogs have gone!' declared the leader of the guard.
Suddenly revitalized by his delight, he pointed to the plumes of dust in the
distance and cursed foully. 'There will be stragglers to kill and slow
wagons to loot. Get after them, in the name of Morocco, and flay the
armour off their pasty backs!'

The thin horses grunted and staggered as Moors sprang into their
saddles and set off in pursuit of the besieging army. Foot-soldiers ran out
and wrenched down the tent, rending it with their teeth and cracking the
tent poles by jumping on them. And when the tent was set ablaze, they
danced round it with the wild chants of African curses in their unfed
mouths. They were still dancing when horses came galloping back
towards the city.

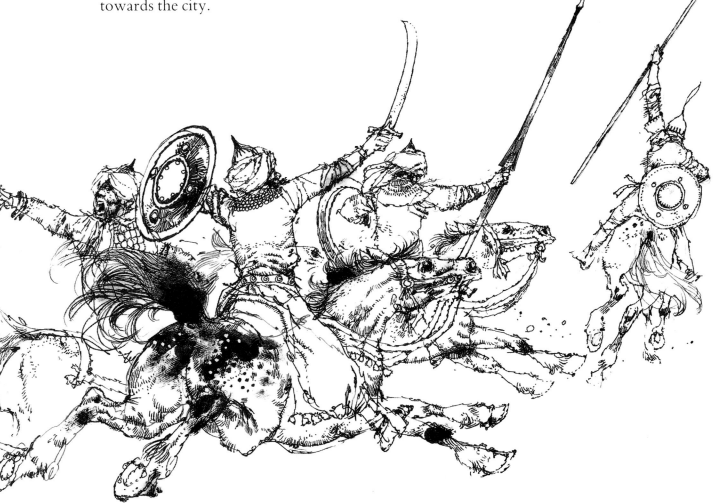

They were not Moorish horses. Don Rodrigo's cavalry from one direction, Alvar Fañez' corps from another struck like arrows falling out of the sun. They pierced the gate in the castle wall left hanging open like an astonished mouth. Not a man rode back into Alcocer that had ridden out of it in such hot pursuit. All that remained of them was a cloud of birds gathering above the horizon and blood on the shoes of Don Rodrigo's horses.

'I claim Alcocer in the name of God and of blessed King Alfonso. May the Lord lay at his feet every such city clutched to the heathen breast of Morocco, and may Don Rodrigo Díaz de Vivar be his instrument!'

'*Amen!*' The harsh shouts from a hundred Castilian throats would have shattered the glass in a cathedral. It shook from the crevices of the city wall a rain of gold and silver coins. Or so it seemed, for the terrified citizens were attempting to buy their lives with fistfuls of money. African coin, Castilian spoil, tributes from Albarracín and Saragossa as well as jewels torn in desperation from helmets and cloaks and sword hilts – they all spilled through the fingers of Rodrigo's men as they gloried in the wealth of Alcocer.

One by one, the riderless horses of the city's army trotted back into the city, calling to the horses in the streets with neighs and hinnies. Empty boots hung in many of their stirrups. Don Rodrigo detached one of these boots as a horse trotted by him, and went to the mountain of loot piled in the street. As he bent down, his chain mail hood fell back from his head, like the skin of a snake being sloughed off as the snake grows greater. Beneath it, his linen coif was creased, and his wiry hair curled in wild disorder round his gaunt face. His beard had grown as thick as a sheep's fleece.

'Alvar Fañez, stand by me!' he said loudly. He knew that every pair of eyes was on the heap of treasure to see how much the Don would take for himself. He filled the Moorish boot and held it up above his head. 'Thirty captured horses I send as tribute to our dear King Alfonso, to show that victory was won in his name! I send them in the keeping of Alvar Fañez who has proved himself my friend and right hand in this battle. And this quantity of battle treasure I send to the Monastery Santa María in Vivar, so that a thousand thanksgivings may be said by the monks for our victory. As for the rest, you may divide it between you equally. While I may eat at the expense of the Moors and shelter in their castles, I need nothing for myself. One tenth part of the spoil I give to Alvar Feñez.'

Alvar Fañez kicked up the dust with the toe of his boot and said softly, 'If it's all the same with you, Don Rodrigo, I shall give my share to your gracious wife and daughters, to comfort them in your absence. Myself, I

want nothing until I've earned it, and this –' (he snapped his fingers in three directions) 'this was no more than washing lice out of my hair. You do me great honour to send me as your messenger into the dear King's presence.'

If Alvar Fañez had his tongue in his cheek, it did not show in his expression or his tone of voice. But when he went to bed that night – a lonely traveller on a lonely road with the champing of thirty-one horses around him in the dark – he did allow himself a moment's misgiving. What kind of welcome lay in store for him at the court of King Alfonso?

The Infantes yapped and yelped round the King's heels. 'What will you do with him? Will you hang him? Will you torture him? Will you send his head back in a bag to the Bastard Rodrigo?'

King Alfonso said nothing. He was intrigued by the news that Alvar Fañez was waiting at the palace gates. What brought a man back to court to the prospect of losing his eyes, his ears, his head, and his right to a Christian burial? Things must be bad indeed for the Don's henchman to be creeping back, cap-in-hand, to throw himself on the King's mercy. Clearly this was Rodrigo's spokesman, come to plead for forgiveness and for shelter from the godless swarming Moors who overran Spain like ants. Somehow Alfonso had not expected such pleas from Don Rodrigo. Somehow he had expected this renowned warrior to accept his fate with dignity and die somewhere in a skirmish.

It would not be courtly to kill the Don's messenger. It would not be kingly to behead Alvar Fañez on the spot. So he called for the man to be allowed to enter the audience chamber, and watched, over superciliously high cheekbones, expecting the criminal to prostrate himself on the floor and writhe. Alvar Fañez went down on one knee, but he certainly did not writhe.

'A thousand prayers are even now hanging between earth and heaven for your health, prosperity and happiness, my lord King, father of all Spain. The lips of priests and soldiers alike call down God's blessing on you night and morning. But the lips of Don Rodrigo Díaz de Vivar, Castejón and Alcocer commend you to God with each hour of the clock, each beat of a bird's wing.'

Alfonso declined his head imperceptibly to acknowledge the greeting. 'Fañez. We recollect your father,' was all he said. (Vivar, Castejón, and Alcocer? What did that mean?)

'I bring from your servant a tribute of thirty horses captured in the taking of Alcocer. My master begs you to know that he conquers only in your name and the name of God Almighty who has graciously smiled on

him since . . . since . . .' Alvar Fañez sheered away from the dangerous word 'exile', 'since he was given the opportunity to plunder the godless Moors. God willing, his enterprises will bring greater tributes in the future. Now, with your permission, I will deliver the Don's greetings to his wife and daughters.'

Alfonso strolled about the room until his casual steps brought him to the window. He idly drew back the curtains with the back of his hand and glanced out at the view. His eyes widened at the sight of the thirty horses in the yard. They were fine Arabian beasts.

'We always liked your father, Alvar Fañez. An excellent soldier. You showed a great deal of . . . *daring*, yes, daring in coming here. We believe We shall pardon you. Yes, We shall. We shall pardon you for disobeying Our decree. You may come and go as you wish. Your life is not forfeit. Pay your respects to the Doña Jimena by all means. We shall not object.'

Alvar Fañez kissed the King's hand with a great deal of feeling. 'And may I take such a message from your lips to brighten my master's life?'

Alfonso snatched his hand away. 'No. We have nothing to say on the subject of that man. He is not spoken of here. Good day, Fañez.'

As Alvar Fañez left the palace, courtiers jostled him on the steps. Outwardly indifferent but inwardly seething with curiosity, they threw questions after him in bored voices. 'So, the Bastard has taken Alcocer, has he?'

'Don Rodrigo Díaz de Vivar has captured Alcocer, yes. And Castejón.'

'With tributes like those horses, the King will be glad he exiled the Bastard.'

'When he sees what tributes follow,' said Alvar Fañez calmly, 'the King may not look kindly on those who insult the honourable Don Rodrigo Díaz.'

They knew he was right. If any more tributes came from the South, the King might choose to forget Rodrigo's offence. The Teifas, the realms of Spain occupied by the Moors, were like dark and deadly mines: a man might fall to his death there, but he might equally grow very rich indeed. The friends of the Don allowed themselves a sigh of relief that he had survived so long. Those who hated him kicked the ground and wished that *they* had thought of raiding a few Moorish border towns.

Doña Jimena said, 'How is he, Alvar? Is he eating enough?'

'Madam, he still eats like a heron. When did he ever look at his plate before a meal or loosen his belt after? All I can say is that his men are eating well and there's plenty of water to wash down the food. You'll like Alcocer.'

'Am I to come now, then?' she asked, gathering her shawls around her as though she were prepared to mount up behind Alvar Fañez.

'No, you must be patient a little while longer. When it is safe, your husband will send for you.'

'The King will never permit it.'

Alvar Fañez closed one eye and looked at her penetratingly with the other.

'God moves in a mysterious way, Doña Jimena de Díaz.'

She looked down into the battered leather boot she was holding, and the gold inside it winked back at her. 'I shall take this money to the monastery myself, and beg God's blessing on you for bringing it. Take care on your journey back to Alcocer. Just tell me again – how does he look?'

'His beard is like the burning bush that spoke to Moses: he has sworn not to cut it until he has won glory in the King's name.'

'Good. It will keep him warm on a winter's night.'

Then Doña Jimena told her women to fill Alvar Fanez' saddlebags with food and wine. She carried the boot of coins up the hill to the monastery. After she had given it to the Abbot she slipped secretly into the chapel. The stones were cold, and an unfriendly draught swirled like water across the paved floor. But when the priests rolled sleepily out of their beds next morning, at the summons of the bell, and shuffled blearily along the slab-cold passageways to the chapel to sing matins, they found the Dona Jimena stretched out on her face, in earnest prayer. She rose unsteadily to her knees, her circulation sluggish with cold. The monks stared, clutching their skirts around them like old washerwomen. But the Abbot went and clasped her hands in his own and said gently, 'You should think of your little girls next time you risk your tender health in such a frosty place.'

'Abbot, doesn't a knight keep vigil on the eve of his knighthood? Doesn't he pray all night for the strength to be worthy?'

'Well, yes.'

'Then I must pray for the strength to be worthy of my husband who will soon be the glory of all Spain!' She paused and then added in a hurry, 'And I must pray for his safety because I know he won't think to do it . . . And I must pray that in all the fury and excitement, he keeps a place in his heart for his wife and children.'

The Abbot laughed. 'Lady. Go home and pack your chests for a journey. Don Rodrigo will surely send for you soon. Without you and the little girls he's a bird without wings, a tree without fruit. Surely he is making a home for you this very moment in Alcocer.'

'Do you really think so. Do you?'

'Why ever not?' said King Mu'taman of Morocco peevishly. 'What is preventing you? Why, if I were to stir myself I could wring that infidel out of Alcocer like the juice out of an orange!' And he brandished in the face of his faithful siddis the letter that had come from the Jalon river valley.

It spoke of an unknown, renegade exile from Castile, a Christian who had taken Alcocer by force and trickery. His success had thrown the nearby towns of Ateca, Terrer and Calatayud into a panic, and it was they who had written to Morocco, to their King, begging his help.

The siddis, Fáriz and Galve, bowed lower and lower until they were lying face-down at the King's feet. 'And so we shall, my Lord. You are the siddi most absolute of every plot of earth created by Allah and kissed by the sun. But Alcocer has *water*, you see! Do not punish our stupidity or sell our wives while we are gone. It will surely take us many months to win victory!'

Beneath the brow band of his burnous, King Mu'taman's black eyes glittered and he bared a fender of huge, glistening teeth. Of all things, he prized subtlety in his military men. As they grovelled in fear, shoulders slumped, foreheads banging on the marble floor, stealing timid glances up at him, he knew full well that they were play-acting.

'Fáriz! Galve! Have your brains dried up in the sun? Can a city not be cut off from its water? Can a siege not be brought quickly to a close? Can a well not be *poisoned*?'

Fáriz and Galve clapped their hands to their heads and rolled their eyes. 'Oh, wonderful!'

'Oh, inspirational!'

'Oh, genius of war!'
'A curse on our teachers that they left us so ignorant!'
'Why did we not think of that, Siddi Galve?'
'Why indeed, Siddi Fáriz?

Siddi Fáriz and Siddi Galve buried a dead horse in the spring which fed the well in Alcocer. It took two days for the putrefaction to creep down the waterway and under the city wall. One morning, a spiral of flies hung in a column of evil-smelling air over the well in the market place. Don Rodrigo de Díaz forbade anyone to drink from it, and summoned the leaders of every detachment to his rooms.

He said, 'I had thought to make a home here, and perhaps to take up tributes from the towns nearby, to keep you in wine and meat and clothing. But it seems that is not to be. Though the food stores are full, our water is poisoned. What for the best, then? To wait until we are shrivelled up like raisins, with our tongues hanging down to our knees? Or to go out now and fight, while we still have sweat to spill?'

There was a great brandishing of swords and baring of teeth. The urge to foray out of the city and fight swept the town like a raging fire. The Moorish members of Rodrigo's army howled and whooped and slapped their bare feet on the stone steps as they ran to the city's battlements to throw curses at the besieging army.

Only then did the enthusiastic noise slack off and die away. Three thousand men were ranged around the city. The banners of Siddis Fáriz and Galve flickered like red tongues whose appetite for blood has been whetted.

El Siddi!

Galve had seen a great monitor lizard lick up frogs from a poolside in his native Africa, frog after frog after . . . a hundred frogs snatched in an afternoon without one being quick enough to escape. He had seen a harvester go out into the field with a scythe and hack down wheat. He had seen the sands of the desert smother a temple tree-high as though it had never been. But he had *never* seen a rout such as Rodrigo Díaz made of his army.

A phalanx of horses gouged a pathway through the Moorish troops without even slowing its speed or breaking stride. The standard-bearer went out ahead, but only as far as a drop of sweat parts from a forehead. Knee to knee and stirrup to stirrup, they streamed out of the gates of the city and reaped the troops of Morocco clear out of their saddles. So sharp were their sword blades that they prised the soul from a man's body like a mussel from its shell, shaved his shadow off the green sleeve of the earth.

When Don Rodrigo had entrusted the banner to Pedro Bermúdez, he had not expected the man to be so *excitable*. No sooner was the pole of it resting in his stirrup and the gate open than he scraped through the gap and charged the enemy screaming, 'There's no going back now! For Rodrigo Díaz de Vivar and for God!' He was a little barrel of a man who bounced in the saddle as a buoy bounces on the sea.

'After him, for pity's sake!' gasped Rodrigo.

And that is how the six hundred chequered troops of the Don came haring out of Alcocer, a tail's length behind Pedro Bermúdez. They clasped their shields to their chests, they ducked their heads and, stirrup to stirrup, knee to knee, they collided with the Moorish army.

Pedro Bermúdez had the banner mounted on the tip of a lance, and he used it to lift various Moors out of their saddles. By the time he was surrounded and in serious danger, the horses of his fellow Castilians, close as the teeth of a comb, were hurling the Moroccans on their heads in the grass. The round, staring shields of the foreigners were blinded by lance points. Coats of mail were torn like paper, and boots hung empty in the stirrups of a thousand riderless horses. Prayers to Muhammad and prayers to Saint James and the name of King Mu'taman and the name of Don Rodrigo Díaz mingled in the air as thick as a flock of scavenging birds.

Martin the Miller went after Galve. As they closed, his lance point missed the siddi's heart. Galve's sword was out: it was too late for Martin to use his. So instead, he brought the shaft of the lance crashing down on the man's helmet. Precious garnets flew in all directions and left the settings in the helmet as ragged as a cheese grater. The siddi's eyes boggled. He was more surprised by the affront than brained by the blow. Then his horse decided the matter by turning on its heels and fleeing the field, as Galve clung on to his saddle with one hand and his head with the other.

Siddi Fáriz saw Don Rodrigo ride at him, his sword flashing through a thousand different arcs, and his own weapon dropped from his hand and he wrenched his horse almost inside out in turning it about. He fled in terror. Once he felt the sword strike sparks off his chain mail. Once he felt the sword slash through his belt and wedge in the saddle behind him. And once he felt a dull, painless blow in the back which he knew was a deep wound. He rode until Calatayud city swelled out of the horizon, and he bellowed himself hoarse in calling for the gates to be opened.

Rodrigo's lance pierced the gate as it closed, and passed right through the splintering wood, where it jammed, twanging with a deep-noted throb. Afterwards, no strength could withdraw it, and it was sawn off short, a reminder to all who came and went of the chase to Calatayud.

Don Rodrigo turned his horse and withdrew before Moorish archers on the wall could let fall a rain of brass-tipped arrows. But Siddi Fáriz, knowing his voice would be heard through the gate, called: 'I pay you tribute, Siddi Rodrigo! Your enemies call you the Bastard, Rodrigo of Alcocer! Your men call you the Conqueror. But I call you *Siddi*! For you are my equal and my match! You have bested me, Siddi Rodrigo! But let all my camels spit on me if there was ever such an army as yours. Allah is in your arm, and none but the magnificent King Mu'taman himself shall put you in your grave!'

Don Rodrigo drew up his horse, even though the arrows were beginning to gouge the dust all around him. He turned his head over his shoulder and said, disdaining to shout, 'With God's grace, only my wife shall do me that favour, señor.' A ripple of astonished laughter and admiration purred along the city wall, and the archers lowered their bows. 'Hail to the Siddi!' they shouted nervously. The Spanish-speakers even strove to compliment Rodrigo in his own language: 'Ola, El Siddi! Viva!'

Suddenly, the shadow of Rodrigo's horse clashed on the ground with the shadow of another, and seemingly from nowhere a rider fell in beside him. 'Well then, hail, El Siddi!'

Rodrigo had half drawn his sword before he recognized the face hidden by the shadow of a Castilian helmet. Then, just for a moment, his impassive features (which in battle had stirred no more than to take breath) broke into a dazzling grin. 'Alvar Fañez! Blessings on all the saints and angels, but I'm glad to see you! Did you reach Vivar?'

'I did, General, I did. And I have to tell you that you're looking at a free man, pardoned fresh from the King's own lips. If I were to tell you the looks on those faces when they heard how we were faring! If you could just have been there when I put that spaniel Manrico in his place – withered him with a glance and a word! You should have been there! And me, I've missed out on something here, I can see. Since when do you start a battle without your faithful right hand, Alvar Fa . . .?'

'No matter! No matter!' Rodrigo's hand reached out and gripped Fañez hard by the arm. 'Tell me quickly: did you see her? Is she well? Is she safe? Is she missing me?'

'Whoever can you mean, General? I just can't think . . . oh, the Doña Jimena, you mean? Well, apart from the wearing out of her poor knees in praying for us all and the wearing out of her petticoat hems in walking up to the monastery every day, she's well enough to outshine the plaster saints and the angels themselves, and that's a fact. She sends word for you to keep warm and remember to eat from time to time.'

'And the girls?'

'Prettier than ever, master. El Siddi, eh? If I could have told them that, how they'd have laughed, the both of them!' And he kicked on his horse and rode just ahead of his general, rather than be thought to have noticed the tears welling up in Don Rodrigo's eyes.

Over the next three years, Don Rodrigo – or El Siddi as he had come to be known – took Monreal and Saragossa, Monzón and Huesa, the Jalón river valley and the Martín, too, even as far as Montalbán, with all the cities that stood along the river banks. Knowing that the water in Alcocer could be poisoned, the place no longer satisfied him as a home for his wife and daughters and he looked to broader and broader horizons for greater and greater achievements. In the end, his mind became set on Valencia, that greatest of all Moorish strongholds, that city of mythical majesty and a splendour only rumoured in the courts of the Christian North.

Rumour was rife at the court of the King. 'They say his army is full of Moors!' 'They say the cities of Teruel and Cella and Saragossa and Montalbán all pay him tribute!' 'They call him El Cid,' they said, inaccurately and elegantly lisping the word in disdainful Castilian.

And Don Rodrigo's friends allowed themselves to smile behind their hands. And those who hated him began to grin loonishly at the King and lisp, 'Ah, was it not your idea to banish the fellow? Was there not something cunning and politic in your justice? Did you not mean him to drive the Moors out of Spain?'

The King even began to wonder himself: 'Did We have it in mind that he might drive the Moors out of Spain? How remarkably wise of Us that would have been!' He kept silent, preferring his court to guess just what

had been in his mind when he banished his finest knight.

Then Alvar Fañez came again, with fifty Arabian horses all saddled in Moroccan leather, with bronze swords hanging from their pommels. The horses' tails were multicoloured with dust from the three different Teifas through which they had passed on the journey, and they snorted with a southern dialect.

'Most exulted Lord! Father of Spain! You are the first thought in the waking mind of my master, the first name mentioned in his prayers. I lay before you the greetings of five hundred men, on behalf of Don Rodrigo Díaz of Vivar and Alcocer, Huesa and Saragossa, Monreal and Jalón. He begs you to accept a further gift of horses in anticipation of the time he can send a gift truly befitting his love for you.' Alvar Fañez bowed very low.

The King's fingers twitched one by one; he was inwardly counting the number of titles after Rodrigo's name. He hovered by the window and looked out at the horses, and his mouth involuntarily shaped itself into a whistle of admiration which he hurriedly turned into a cough. 'Look here, Fañez . . .' He glanced around him, and found that the walls of the audience chamber were suddenly lined with nonchalant courtiers who had strayed in behind Alvar Fañez and were now standing about with looks of profound indifference on their faces, one ear strained towards the King. Certain counts and barons were strutting up and down the room, scorning to hover, but pausing to lend an ear every time they passed by. Count Ordoñez was among them. Alfonso scowled. 'We thank you, Alvar Fañez, for bringing this tribute of horses. It is, you may say, not an entirely unacceptable gift. Tell Us, if you will, are We to believe the wild and extravagant rumours that reach Us on every southern wind? Is it true that a one-time acquaintance of this court has captured *five* cities in the occupied Teifas?'

'Oh fourteen, sir, but I didn't like to trouble you with the others; some of them are only little.' Alvar Fañez found himself risen off his knees; he dropped back down apologetically.

'*Fourtee . . .!*'

'Huh. If that barbarous scoundrel can do it, this killing of Moors must be an easy thing,' said the Count Ordoñez in a loud voice saturated with scorn. The King steadied himself.

'Fourteen? And pray, is it true that he means to besiege Valencia?'

'Unless his King forbids it,' said Fañez humbly.

Alfonso hopped about excitedly. 'Forbid? No, no, no, he must . . . That's to say, We do not concern Ourselves with the foolhardiness of exiles. He may conduct himself as he chooses. . . . Has he got enough men to do it?' The King could not help himself; his curiosity was stronger than his aplomb.

Alvar Fañez spread his hands, 'With God's help all things are possible. But if God would arrange for a few more men to join us, it would be useful.'

The King's eyes darted about the room. The courtiers had edged away from the wall to catch more of the conversation, and appeared to be closing in. The counts and barons had stopped strutting to listen. Alfonso stroked his moustache and raised his voice for their benefit. 'This is somewhat in keeping with Our hopes. We are not displeased. Furthermore, We decree that no man of Castile shall forfeit life or land who joins in the siege of Valencia. For three centuries the heathen Moors have occupied God's Spain. God grant that Our reign shall see an end to that occupation!'

Alvar Fañez was off his knees again. 'And Don Rodrigo Díaz himself, your Majesty? Is he forgiven?'

Just as the King opened his mouth to speak, his eye was caught by the Count Ordoñez, scarlet in the face, his jowls flapping like an angry turkey, as he jabbed a finger into his beard and made little tugging gestures to commemorate Rodrigo's heinous crime.

'Of him We have nothing to say,' said the King, thrusting his nose towards Heaven and heading for the door as fast as he could go with dignity.

Pandemonium broke out in the hall after the King had left it. The court was split down the middle, between those who wanted to join El Cid and those whose jealous loathing for the man grew with every breath of his triumphs. They argued and ranted their way out of doors into the dismal rainy courtyard, and left Alvar Fañez crouched on hands and knees, exhausted, in the centre of the room.

Only two figures remained in the room with him, lurking by the long, panelled curtains. The Infantes, Diego and Fernando, sidled closer; Alvar gradually became aware of their thin, stockinged legs and a strong smell of the dried rose petals stuffed inside their breeches. A ringed hand rested lightly on his back. 'Don Alvar! Sir! A favour, I pray!'

A shudder ran through Fañez. He could not understand why. 'I have to be getting back to Don Rodrigo's camp,' he said.

'The merest nothing!' cried Diego with a flourish of one hand. 'Will you favour us by carrying a simple thought to your esteemed and valiant master?'

'Simply remember us to him!' declared Fernando with an extravagant bow to nobody in particular. 'And if you were to mention to him what noble, lusty, and presentable fellows we seemed when you saw us – well, there might be a hundred marks in it for you.'

'Do you want to come and fight with us, then?' asked Alvar Fañez disbelievingly.

'No,' said both the Infantes quickly. 'But we might one day think of presenting ourselves . . . of offering ourselves . . . as suitors to the glorious, ethereal, sublime daughters of his loins, Doña Sol and Doña Elvira.' Fernando darted his face in close against Alvar's: 'What do you think he'd say?'

Alvar Fañez' jaw dropped and he was horrified to find all their four hands pushing money into his various pockets. He pulled free of them and struggled to think of the correct thing to say. 'I'll ask him. I can't say. I don't know! Elvira? Little Sol? Good Lord in Heaven! What an extraordinary thing. I'll certainly mention you to him. Yes, yes. I promise to do that. But I really must be going!' And overcome by a sudden inexplicable panic, Alvar Fañez gathered up his saddlebags and ran.

The Price of Freedom

The Teifa of Albarracín, the Teifa of Saragossa, and the Teifa of Lérida were set rattling like the plates on a table when a great dog leaps up for its supper. The noise of siege and foray, skirmish and pitched battle echoed in the mouths of frightened messengers riding from city to city. Dismay spread among the Moors in Spain. The rumours stretched as far afield as Morocco itself, and through those districts of Spain *not* in Moorish hands. For instance, the long-leaved trees in the Spanish-held realm of Barcelona shook with the racketing up and down and the battle cry of *'God and El Cid!'*

'Who? What? Who is this *'Cid'* marauding along my fences?' demanded Count Ramón Berenguer, a bullying man with bulging eyes, and cheeks mapped over with purple veins.

'He used to be Don Rodrigo Díaz de Vivar and a knight of King Alfonso,' his spy informed him, reading the information off cuffs and off scraps of paper tucked about his person. 'He was exiled for insulting . . .'

'I know him! Do I pay you to tell me what I know? I *know* Rodrigo Díaz. I knew him when he was a scrawny, chicken-legged squire straight off the pig farm! When he was a guest in my castle, he punched my nephew and knocked him down – and him deserving twice the respect, being twice as old as the Díaz boy. Is that brat "El Cid?" I should have drowned him in a bucket then and there. Does he dare to come threatening my borders? Does he mean to pirate my land from under me? I should have drowned him in a bucket, I tell you, while I had him under my roof!'

A shower of notes and wax seals fell to the floor as the spy rolled up his sleeves and trouser legs in search of more intelligence. 'He hasn't said . . . he's never suggested . . . he always claims that he has no claim on Barcelona, your lordship . . .'

'Well of course he means to have it. Now that he's flexed his muscles he'll reach and reach until he overreaches himself and tries to steal Barcelona. Well I won't sit here idly waiting. I won't stand by and give him the advantage. I'll put that upstart peasant in his place. This is what comes of knighting peasants. I trust Alfonso will learn by it! *Call out the troops!*'

When Don Rodrigo heard about the Count's anger (and he could not fail to hear, for every hole hammered out by the woodpeckers that spring seemed to shout it, and every crocus grew striped with purple, like the Count's face), he wrote a letter:

My dearly respected and most revered Count. I beg you to set your mind at rest when you hear of my modest exploits in the Teifas which border on your land. Think merely that I am driving troublesome cats out of your neighbour's garden. My army shall set no foot in your territory. My eyes are set only on driving the Moors out of God's holy Spain and in finding some pleasant quarter where my little family can live out its days. I beg you, rather than mistrust me, to take joy in my work and my triumphs over the invaders from Morocco.

Remembering your hospitality in my youth, I esteem myself fortunate if I may account myself your friend and brother Christian.

The messenger did not have far to carry the letter. Over the second little hill beyond Don Rodrigo's camp he came across the Count of Barcelona and a thousand troops ranged for battle.

The Count Ramón in his armour, like a great shiny bucket over a well, was being lowered by a winch on to his horse. When he saw the messenger coming, wearing the Don's crest on his tabard, he pointed so excitedly that he set himself spinning on the end of the rope.

The messenger took one look at the battle array, threw the letter in the general direction of the Count, then turned and rode off at the speed of thought, flattening himself along his horse's neck.

'Take him! Hunt him down like a dog!' bawled the Count, rattling and buckling with rage. 'Everyone after him! A hundred marks for his head and his horse!' The Count's squires deserted the winch and left Ramón dangling, spinning and cursing, as they joined in the chase. A

Moorish slave, thinking to furl the Count's tent for battle, let go of the wrong rope, so that the suspended man plunged down into his saddle, winding his horse which stood snorting and sagging.

When he reached his saddle, the Count sat in it like a man in a bath, slumped back with his feet out in front. And like a man settling into his bath who watches the water slop forward and overspill, he felt a satisfaction that eased the pain. His army, dazzling bright under the spring sun, washed forward ahead of him and disappeared over the brow of the hill. He trotted gently after them, content to miss the early, most robust fighting. The rope from the winch, still knotted round his chest, trailed after him across the grass.

He topped the rise and watched the two armies close, all in among El Cid's unprepared tents, carts and wagons. Ramón's fist plunged repeatedly into his saddle leather as he muttered, 'That's it. Get in there. Smash them. Slaughter them. Crush them. Good. Excellent!' After all these years, he could still pick out the figure of Rodrigo Díaz de Vivar – a forked wraith of a man sitting bolt upright in the saddle, turning his horse solely with his knees, a single mailed hand resting lightly on the reins. With the other he hacked and slashed and thrust and parried and wheeled and struck, making ground and rallying his men to it, clearing the tents and clearing the wagons, advancing and advancing and . . .

The Count of Barcelona hauled on his reins so hard that his horse bent double in turning round. And the sound of his armour's clattering, as he bounced about in the saddle, frightened grouse out of the heather. He looked around him like a naked man in need of pockets. His tent alone had not been fully collapsed ready for battle. As he galloped past it, the trailing rope around his chest tangled with the guy ropes and all of a sudden Ramón's tailbone hit the back of his saddle, the horse's rump, and the ground in quick succession. His horse gave not a backward glance, but speeded up considerably.

When Don Rodrigo, cresting the rise, surveyed the dismantled camp site of his ambushers, only one tent was still partially raised. Its conical shape slumped sideways like a limp nightcap, and the Count of Barcelona's pennant licking the ground. With the tip of his lance, Don Rodrigo lifted an unfastened flap.

'Good day to you, Count. I entreat you to permit me to offer you the hospitality of my supper and my tent.'

Beneath the sagging brocade canopy, his round body propped up on a knoll of richly embroidered cushions and his short legs crossed nonchalantly at the ankles, sat the Count of Barcelona, his long hair combed forward over one shoulder. His cheeks were strangely red in contrast with the whiteness of his face in general – as if he had been pinching them to restore the colour. On hearing the Don's invitation, he coughed once to lower his voice and replied, 'Sir. Do I look like a man who eats with dogs? You have scored a victory over me, I cannot deny it. But I can deny you the pleasure of seeing me beg for my life!'

The Castilian pushed back his chain-mail balaclava: the linen coif beneath it fell creased across his shoulders. 'My dear Count. If you grant my simple requests, we shall have no need to talk of such things.'

Ramón fingered his hair and examined the back of one hand. 'Hear this, cur. Sooner than grant you the smallest favour, my mouth shall remain shut. No morsel of food shall pass my lips, nor no plea for mercy either. Do your worst. Though you torture me, I shall never submit. You are the bastard son of a peasant and it demeans me even to address you.'

El Cid wrinkled up his weather-beaten eyes and seemed about to speak again. But then he simply bowed from the saddle and let the tent flap fall back. 'Pedro Bermúdez, escort the gentleman to my tent. He is my guest, you understand? Treat him courteously.'

The scene in Rodrigo's tent that night was one of unrivalled delight. Instead of the dank and dismal smells that usually greeted them after they had besieged and conquered some little town, there was only the scent of the evening breeze blowing pollen into the sunset, the smell of roasting lamb and beef on spits, and the heavy, wholesome smell of the horses moving about in the gloom. They parted the defeated army of Barcelona from silver, gold, weapons, and tents, but fed them too (albeit off their own meat) and let them drown their sorrows in vats of their own Barcelona wine.

The flaps of the Don's tent were thrown up, so that the light of the little Moorish lamps spilled out to meld with the glare of oily torches stuck in the soft ground. Under the largest lamp, still king of his castle of cushions, sat Ramón, Count of Barcelona, his hands nonchalantly pressed against his stomach to keep it from rumbling. His eyelids were closed, and a thin moustache of sweat lay along his top lip which he moistened from time to time with the tip of his tongue.

Inside his head were pictures of his headless body sprawled in a ditch, his own face peering out through the bars of a cage, his whole family walking in chains through the streets of Barcelona. What shocking fate did this barbarous son of a peasant have in store for him, apart from stealing his realm? The monster would undoubtedly kill him and all his family, whether or not Ramón signed away his power. He scorned, therefore, to make any act of surrender. Let El Cid steal the land from him: he would never part with it willingly.'

He opened his lashes just wide enough to see his beautiful tooled leather boots, and his throat crammed with tears at the thought of being parted from them by death. Never to pull them on again on a bright morning! Never to have his pretty wife pull them off again at night! Bravery did not come easily to Count Ramón.

'My dear Count, I beg you! Don't blight our celebrations with a long face!' cried Don Rodrigo from the other side of the tent. He was watching his men dancing and feasting and his face wore a look of profound contentment. 'I told you before, grant me one favour – just one – and you may leave here unharmed, unmolested. One little favour. One small boon. I regret that I shall have to keep any money your army was carrying – to defray expenses, you understand. Such an expensive business, this driving out of Moors. But grant me one wish and you shall be rewarded with your freedom.'

'One favour, eh? My realm, I suppose. The surrender of my realm. Never! You may take Barcelona from me, but I shall never give it to you! I am ready for your headsman!'

In three paces Rodrigo crossed the tent and squatted down on his long legs in front of Ramón to clap both hands round the man's shoulders. 'My Lord Count! Your realm? Did I not send word to you that I have no wish nor ambition to attack Barcelona? There are Moors enough in Spain without I make war on a Christian province or steal land from a Christian gentleman! No! All I ask is that you *join in our feasting*!'

'*That's the favour*?'

'That's the favour. What? Did you think I was going to ask you to give me Barcelona? Ha ha! No! But if you eat well enough and drink deep enough, you are free to go, and Barcelona shall never see a whisker of my beard!'

The platelets of Ramón's armour heaved and twitched, as if a giant crab were trying to slough off its shell. 'If I thought for one moment that you'd keep your word . . .'

Ramón saw the backbone stiffen, the colour drain out of Don Rodrigo's face, and his sun-bleached eyebrows rise as though to escape the shock in his eyes. 'Sir! In all my life I have *never* broken my word!'

The Count wallowed a little in his effort to get up out of the cushions. His bulk was against him. 'Well, send in the food, man! I could eat the King of Morocco and all his horses!'

Supper was brought on a great silver gilded tray taken from Saragossa: two chickens and a side of lamb, with fruit and vegetables and sauces as thick and hot as volcanic lava. And Count Ramón ate it till the grease dripped off his elbows, pausing only once, to wipe gravy off his tooled leather boots. He washed it down with three bottles of wine which chased the blood round his body until it caught up with his brain. Outside, night rubbed thin, and morning showed through. When at last he finished, he pulled out a huge white handkerchief from his doublet, and wiped his face and beard. 'By the Feast of Christmas, food's not tasted that good for a life and a half! Have I granted your favour, *El Cid*?'

'Twice over, sir! Now you'll want to sleep off that meal before we go our separate ways.'

Ramón shot him a look of vilest distrust, then said airily, 'No, no, I think I'd rather be on my way now. *At once.*'

So Rodrigo called for horses to be brought, and rode beside Ramón to the borders of Barcelona's realm. On the journey, the Count groaned only very occasionally with indigestion.

At the river which separated the Teifa of Lerida from Barcelona, Rodrigo drew out from beside his saddle the Count's own sword. At the sight of its naked blade Ramón flinched in terror and his eyes bulged. He plunged his horse into the river, clinging round its neck as it was washed downstream, then scrambled ashore on the far side.

'My dear Count,' called Rodrigo anxiously. 'I only wished to return your sword. It's a fine weapon. It must be worth a thousand marks at least.'

'Keep it, El Cid. Keep it! It's name's Colada and it's solid Moorish silver and I wish you joy of it.' Slowly he realized that Rodrigo had no intention of pursuing him across the river to cut his throat, and he sniggered as he looked down at his dripping, sodden clothes. 'I see now you are a man of your word, Don Rodrigo Díaz de Vivar! I shall let the whole world know it!'

Don Rodrigo bowed from the saddle 'Please don't give me cause to empty your pockets again, Count Ramón – I like you far too much.'

'Don't you worry, El Cid! Much as I honour you, I'll be happy if I never set eyes on you again. Well, where will your crusade take you next? The sea? Will you conquer the realms of the deep now?'

Don Rodrigo ran his hand down the length of his beard, as if in thought. 'I thought perhaps Valencia,' he called quietly.

The Count burst out laughing with a violence that shook his horse. 'Valencia! By the Angel Michael! Why tickle the Moor's ribs when you can tear out his heart, eh? I admire you, El Cid! Your father only strove to be a knight: you want to be a martyr! Goodbye – And if you storm Valencia, I'll see you next in Heaven!'

The look of astonishment never quite left Count Ramón's ruddy face, and whenever he recounted the story of his defeat, no one was left in any doubt that El Cid was a remarkable, nay superhuman, man. In fact, it came to be believed that he stood taller than a camel's jaw, wore armour dipped in the waters of holy Bethesda Pool, and a coif under his helmet made of Christ's table linen at the Last Supper. Light escaped round the sides of his breastplate, and his horse could talk. If Ramón did not start the rumours, he certainly did not discourage them: it became something of a privilege even to have met El Cid, let alone been beaten by him. According to Ramón, glory ran down off Rodrigo Díaz de Vivar and left gold in his horse's hoof prints.

And at the mention of gold, young men throughout Spain saddled up, kissed their mothers, and went to join the army of El Cid the Conqueror. El Cid's eyes were set on Valencia, stronghold of the Moors, and inside Valencia were untold hoards of treasure for the sharing. All Spain knew that. Even at the court of King Alfonso, some young men were itching to go and lap up the glittering trail of El Cid.

But that was one thought which never crossed the minds of the Infantes Diego and Fernando. In three years they had grown from obnoxious children into obnoxious young men. But fighting Moors held no appeal for them. They could inflict pain on servants and squires whenever they fancied, and as for the glory of battle, they preferred the glory gained from wearing a new suit of clothes and strutting up and down while the pretty girls stared.

'Of course, if the Bastard takes Valencia, he'll be the richest man in Christendom,' said Diego. 'The King is bound to pardon him.'

'Yes, but to marry his daughters!'

'Could we really lower ourselves and marry those yokel brats?'

'They're twelve. They're women now, almost. Have you seen them?' and he whistled suggestively.

'Yes, but marry a *Díaz*. The shame! It'd be like marrying into the pig house. This is Rodrigo Díaz of Vivar we're talking about, you know — well-known bastard and hick farmer.'

And seeing the curl of his brother's lip, Diego nodded and scratched himself through his velvet. 'You're right, of course. The shame would kill us . . . Anyway, he'll die at Valencia.'

'The shame! Oh Allah in Heaven, the shame and the gall!' roared King Mu'taman beating his breast. 'This Siddi has made a laughing stock of my generals and cohorts! Will no one stand and face this expansionist infidel, this pirate, this outcast from his own kind? Now his eyes are set on

Valencia – my crown in Spain! – and does Allah not strike him dead for the blasphemy? Aie! Aie! El Siddi at the gates of Valencia and at my own back the Rif are overrunning my oases.' He swept a furious outstretched arm in the direction of the ninety ministers trembling face-down on the marble floors. 'If I were free to set sail now, I would show you *single-handed* how to cut a Christian throat! They may call him Siddi, but his blood is the milky mush of a common Christian. Don't let it come to my ears that he has taken Valencia. Woe and pain on him who tells me such news!'

Whipping his robes around his legs with a menacing crack, he stalked out of their presence. Just outside the room, he dipped his fingers in rosewater and wiped them delicately on a towel. He said quickly and calmly to his body slave, 'Keep me informed please. I may need to fight Don Rodrigo after these wars at home are out of the way.'

'I wish mother didn't cry so often,' said Elvira. She and her sister stood face to face, plaiting each other's hair. 'Why does she do it, I wonder, and always when she thinks no one is looking?'

'It's about Father, I expect. I expect it upsets her when people keep calling him *El Cid*. It's a very silly name if you ask me.'

'She says it means "Lord" in Morocco. But he isn't Moroccan, is he?

Or do you suppose his face has turned black now with being under the southern sun so much?'

'Sometimes I can't remember his face, you know,' said Sol penitently. 'Is that wicked?'

'I hope not. 'Cos I can't remember it either – except sometimes when I dream of him.'

The sisters both sighed deeply and sat down, their half-braided hair unwinding in their laps.

'What do you dream, Elvira?'

'I dream I'm in Valencia. Mother says it has roofs of glass held up by a thousand pillars of marble inlaid with magic signs, and fountains of water just running to waste on every corner. She says every house has a garden and a silver balcony – and there are stone walls as loopy as lace and gates worked in filigree like whole nests of copper snakes – and towers as thin as fingers and tall as the sky . . . Do you suppose he'll come back one day with lots of money and presents for us?'

'I'd like a cloak embroidered with silver and with garnets round the collar – and a muff made out of lion's fur! Will he bring us things like that, do you suppose, Elvira?'

'Oh he'll bring us better than that,' said Elvira, finishing off her plait with briskly efficient fingers. Her eyes glowed. 'He'll bring us both a dowry that will buy us two knights for husbands – or counts! Or maybe even siddis from over the ocean!'

'Elvira! What are you saying! A siddi? He'd have a black face and a crooked sword and . . . and he wouldn't be a *Christian*! No, I want someone like . . .' Sol blushed and dropped her eyes as though she had let slip a secret.

Elvira was intrigued. 'Who, Sol? Like who? Oh, do say, little Soletta!'

'Shshsh. It's silly. You'll laugh at me. Someone like . . . Fernando de Carrión . . . Not that I've ever spoken to him, of course.'

'The Infante! My!'

Sol looked up with wide, shining eyes. 'He wears such *beautiful* clothes, and he's as grand as a peacock, and that roan horse of his is almost purple and . . . and he's really quite handsome.'

'If it weren't for the ears,' said Elvira thoughtfully. She affected a very casual tone when she said, 'To look at I prefer his brother, Diego, myself. Not that I've ever spoken to him, of course.' And flicking her plait over her shoulder, she dismissed the idea as foolish. 'We're dreaming, Sol. Valencia's a dream. And if Father would just come home, I wouldn't care what he brought with him.'

'Me neither,' said Sol.

The Spoils
of
Valencia

Just as the Great Flood brought Noah's ark at long last to the summit of the highest mountain, so time and a great outpouring of blood brought El Cid at last to the walls of Valencia.

Jérica, Onda and Almenara, all of Burriana, Murviedro, and Cebolla fell to him. And though Valencia sent its own army to turn him back, it might as well have hurled rocks at a rising tide. Their tent poles were broken, their brocaded tents slumped in the mud and their banners licked the ground in defeat. Only the city itself remained to fall.

Three years and a great outpouring of blood brought El Cid to the walls of Valencia. When he came, orange trees were smothering the plain with blossom as far as the eye could see but for the hazy blue crescent of the sea beyond. Patient and placid and cheerful, El Cid besieged Valencia, stronghold of the Moors. He sat his army down around the city, beneath the orange trees. He sank the boats by which the people of the city might send for help to Africa. He dammed the River Turia, which flowed

through the city, to a muddy trickle. And he sent word to all the cities he had conquered and ransomed: 'If there are any among you who wish to join Rodrigo Díaz the Conqueror, called El Cid, the table is wide enough, the feast is great enough and the welcome will be warm enough. Come black, come white, come Arab stallion and Christian mare. The treasure-house of the Moors is ripe for the picking.'

With every week, the oranges formed and swelled and turned from green to gold. And so the army of El Cid swelled and swelled, like a woman awaiting a birth, and in the ninth month it stirred itself.

One January morning, after nine months of siege, when the orange trees were bare, the siegers woke to see Valencia crystallize out of the morning mists as it did each morning. Like a golden honeycomb built by bees out of the honey sunshine, it gradually became visible. Their wonder never lessened at the sight of the needle-thin minarets, the domes of brass and glass, the overlapping, lip-red roofs of the pure white houses piled up and up and up . . . But this morning, like seagulls scavenging over a great dead whale, flapped a hundred white flags of surrender, and the gate stood open. Even the smell of hunger and filth and suffering inside was masked by the perfume of its gardens and flowery balconies.

Rodrigo Díaz ran his hand down his beard: it reached now to the middle of his breastbone and was bleached by the sun even in winter. He said to himself, 'This is the home for my wife and daughters. This befits them.'

Alvar Fañez and Pedro Bermúdez and Martin the Miller were all mounted and raring to see inside the city walls. When Pedro overheard his general's words, he could contain himself no longer. Beneath him his horse pranced wildly, and all at once he shouted, 'Valencia for El Cid! Valencia for El Cid!'

'Silence!' Rodrigo commanded. 'Don Pedro, what are you thinking of?' He raised his voice, though it seemed to cost him some effort. 'If you please: Valencia for God and the King of Spain – for God and King Alfonso. Now, shall we enter?'

The starving and terrified people of the city squatted on their balconies and threw down coins and flowers, flowers and coins. There was a noticeable shortage of horses and cats and dogs in the city, a surplus of bones in the midden, and too many graves under the wall. But the works of three hundred years of Moorish occupation glittered in untarnished perfection all along the banks of the River Turia. Palm trees erupted in tropical exuberance, darkest green against the pale sky. Rising in his stirrups, Don Rodrigo cried, 'I give to every man of my army a house of

his own, that he may send for his family and live here in this city of perpetual summer!'

The cheer that went up was muted. The Castilians cluttering up the narrow streets in their torn clothes and dusty boots, straddling unkempt horses and watched by a thousand frightened pairs of dark eyes in a thousand cloth-wrapped faces, were cowed by the sheer outlandish beauty of Valencia. The air was dented with Muhammadan prayers, like hammered brass. They might just as well have been in Africa.

'I'm going home,' one man whispered to his friend. 'As soon as he's shared out the treasure, I'm off home. This is no place for a Christian man.'

Alvar Fañez looked around him and saw the same words in the mouths of a hundred different man. In the very month of Rodrigo's victory, his army was threatening to melt away like snow under this brassy, southern sky. He looked to see if Don Rodrigo had noticed the change come over his men. The Conqueror was still standing in his stirrups: 'One of these days, the King of Morocco will stir himself and see that his richest possession has fallen into our hands. Then there will be a fight – by my sword! – a fight like the colliding of Africa and Spain! If any man does not have the courage to stay and defend Valencia against King Mu'taman, he is perfectly free to go: I fully understand. He shall have his share of treasure and his share of glory. All I ask is that he bids me goodbye in person and kisses my hand before he abandons me. For it would not be the act of a gentleman to creep away in secret.'

Alvar Fañez smiled. Rodrigo had known Castilians all his life: he knew their weaknesses. He used their sense of honour to shame them into being loyal.

Only one building in Valencia was derelict. The Cathedral of Saint Estabán, scorned by the occupying Moors, had no roof, and sea birds had nested on the high altar. Grass grew between the paving slabs, and ivy strangled the broken pillars. Someone had smashed the faces of the plaster saints, and the noses were chipped off the tombs of the dead. Such sacrilege and neglect was enough to dismay even Don Rodrigo. How could he ask Jimena, Elvira, and Sol to come to such a heathen place?

Suddenly a high tenor voice ricocheted down the street like a sharp stone, and a man straddling a donkey and dragging his feet in the dust came trotting through the ranks, singing in quacking Barcelona Latin. He stopped at the bottom of the steps of Saint Estabán cathedral, and peered short-sightedly at Don Rodrigo. 'Ah! It must be you. I can tell by the beard. He said it was a beard and a half. I'm Don Pedro, Abbot of the Monastery of San Jerónimo in Barcelona. Your good friend Count Ramón

sends his well wishes for the taking of Valencia . . . but I see that you already took it, so I'll give you his congratulations instead. And if you let me, I'm your man to knock the heathen dust out of the place and shout the name of God in its ears . . . By Saint Jude, what's this ruin of a church? Let me at it. Wait till I lay hands on the blasphemous rogues who did this damage. By Holy Peter, send me a pot of paint and a stonemason! Out of my way, you Castilian fops. Ah, Moors! Good strong Moors! Give me them for my workmen El Cid, and I'll give you a cathedral to praise God in inside a month. Cut my ears off if I don't – and off my donkey, too!'

The mood eased like a rope going slack. Men began laughing. Don Rodrigo pushed back his chain-mail hood, and the linen coif beneath it outshone the white seagull chased off the high altar by the wild Abbot Pedro.

Rodrigo made him Abbot of Valencia, and sent thanks to Count Ramón. He loosed the city's thin and starving horses out on to the green plain, and when they were fat and sleek, he saddled them in red Moroccan leather and accoutred them for war with weapons from the Moorish armoury. Then he said to Alvar Fañez: 'Go to Valencia and ask the dear King – beg him to accept these horses and to look kindly on the unworthy subject who sends them. Tell him Valencia has fallen. It is in Christian hands again and it is a fit place for womenfolk. Ask him . . . beg him, if you have to . . . to let the Doña Jimena and my daughters join me in exile here, and the waiting-women of Vivar as well. Tell him that if loneliness is a scourge then I have been soundly punished for my offences.' Rodrigo's fingers bit deep into his lieutenant's arm. 'Just tell him, Alvar Fañez. Just tell him to let my wife come.'

'And what shall I tell Diego and Fernando?' said Fañez. Ever since his return he had been trying to wring an answer out of Don Rodrigo. Every time, he had pretended not to hear the question or changed the subject or sunk deep into thought.

The fingers dropped away from Alvar Fañez' arm. A strange shadow stole across the back of Rodrigo's eyes. 'The Infantes? An answer. Yes, they must be answered. A compliment indeed. Infantes for little Sol and Elvira. . . . It's just that they were such . . . such very *graceless* boys . . .'

'People change. People grow up,' said Fañez with a shrug. 'Your daughters are almost fourteen now. I dare swear you remember them as eight-year-olds.'

El Cid looked suddenly gloomy. He picked up the tip of his magnificent beard and examined the streaks of grey. 'I missed their flowering,' he said, but only his lips moved. Then he threw up his head and scowled. 'No, no. They're too young. My compliments to the noble Infantes, but you may tell them, if they ask, that my daughters are too young to marry. Go on, then. Go!'

Let Allah, the one true God, be praised throughout the world. The Arabic ciphers crawled like a million exquisite scorpions up the walls and pillars of King Mu'taman's halls. Inlaid in ivory on thornwood panels, or jet black stone in marble, there was not a hand's breadth between the columns of lettering which climbed the walls and smothered the ceiling in prayer. Nowhere could a man look without seeing the upward torrent of prayer and praise teeming up and over him – unless he sank his eyes in the silken pile of the carpeted floor.

King Mu'taman was weary. He had driven the rebellious Rif back into their arid mountains, but he was well aware that a man who seeks to sweep clean the desert will wear out a multitude of brushes in one lifetime. Now Valencia had fallen. Across the sea, on the green plain of orange trees, the legendary 'El Siddi' had taken Valencia. All of Allah's Spain was falling, falling, falling into the hands of Christian heathens. Mu'taman lifted his eyes up off the floor, and the words decorating the walls and the ceiling nagged him unmercifully. *Let Allah, the one true God, be praised throughout the world.*

'Let the tents be folded. Let the tent poles be tied in bundles. Let nine hundred ships be made ready and call on all my armies to muster by the

sea. Now I shall break El Siddi like a stick of cinnamon. Like a scarab beetle I shall tread upon him!'

But the dark cloud did not lift off his heart when he had said the words. He wondered why. The words on the walls and ceiling looked suspiciously like a list of his sins and shortcomings: *Let Allah, the one true God, be praised throughout the world.*

'Damn him! Damn him to hell,' said Fernando, kicking the leg of a chair. 'What does he mean, "they're too young"? Does he keep his chickens till they're only good for boiling? The arrogance of the bastard! Does he think he'll get another offer like ours for his scrawny daughters? Well, good riddance. Never wanted them anyway.'

Diego scowled and sighed. He had wanted to stab Alvar Fañez for bringing the insult of a refusal. But there never seemed to be a moment when the wretched yokel was not surrounded by inquisitive and fawning noblemen. Diego hated his brother for suggesting the marriage to Sol and Elvira in the first place. He shut his ears to the talk buzzing along every corridor of Valencia's treasure spilling into the streets, and of palaces for the asking and of year-round sunshine. He put his fingers in his ears while King Alfonso addressed the court.

'Noblemen! Subjects of Our Royal Person! Heralds and chroniclers, take note!' said Alfonso grandly to silence the hubbub in the audience chamber. He smiled beamingly. 'Our loyal friend, Don Alvar Fañez, has come with long-awaited news. Valencia has fallen to Don Rodrigo the Conqueror, called "El Cid". Now it may be revealed that this was Our will. It was with Our blessing that Don Rodrigo began his great and heroic crusade into the territories of the godless! We hoped all along for this!'

Alvar Fañez' jaw dropped. From his familiar position, on his knees in front of the throne, he looked around him and saw the same astonishment written on every other face in the room. The Count Ordõnez' pomaded hair was shaking like a thundercloud, and scattered wisps of darkness down into his face.

'So he's pardoned, then?' squeaked Fañez in the silence that followed the gasps.

'Naturally!'

'And his lands . . .'

'Are restored to him, of course . . . Though We dare to hope that he will make his home in Valencia now, and defend it against the vengeance of King Musselman.'

'Mu'taman,' whispered Alfonso's adviser behind his sleeve, but the King was in no mood to be corrected.

'We urge his wife, his daughters and all his household to travel to

Valencia, each one bearing a gift of greetings from a proud King! Arise, Sir Alvar Fañez! And when you see . . . El Cid, ha, ha . . . El Cid, tell him that We thank him most heartily for fulfilling Our command. All Spain thanks him. Indeed. Yes.' A slight blush colouring his cheeks, King Alfonso hurriedly left the room. When the furious Count Ordoñez demanded a private audience, he was told that the King was busy inspecting his new horses and would not be available for the rest of the day.

Alvar Fañez stood up and again looked around him at the faces in the gloomy, oak-lined chamber. The yellow and smoke-stained faces of gilt-framed portraits looked down scornfully on the babble of noblemen arguing below:

'He never told us.'

'He let us weep for him and his family.'

'He let us think he was an exile, banished on pain of death!'

'So the beard-pulling was just an excuse: the King put him up to it.'

'Why him? Why not send one of us?'

Just for a moment, Alvar Fañez had doubts himself. Perhaps Don Rodrigo had been under the King's command all along. Then he thought of Doña Jimena and of Sol and Elvira and of the look in Rodrigo's eyes when they were mentioned. And he knew that nothing but exile could have kept the father apart from his family. The dark, gossip-filled room seemed suddenly ice-cold, and Alvar longed to go back south to the sun and the open places of Valencia.

He rode full tilt to Vivar and spilled his news at Doña Jimena's feet. 'Your husband is pardoned! I've come to fetch you! You're free to join him! The King gives his consent! You don't need to pack much: Valencia has everything! Bring the household, too. I'm to tell you to bring all your waiting-women. Shut up the house and lease the farm! Where are the girls? How many horses do you own? Send to the monastery to tell the Abbot. Can you be ready in two days, my lady? El Cid will skin me alive if I waste time getting you there!'

Doña Jimena did not seem to hurry. She laid down her sewing beside her in the window seat. She stood up and closed the shutters across the window. She rang an almost inaudible handbell, and quiet-footed women slipped softly into the room. 'It is time,' she said, and they began to take down the curtains and lay them over the furniture. They lifted a small chest from the recess beside the fire and carried it into the garden where a donkey and three horses had shambled from somewhere to eat the lupins and goldenrod. The only noise was a clatter on the stairs as Sol and Elvira ran, unaware and chattering, into the living room. 'Daughters, it is time,' said

their mother. Dartingly the girls clasped each other's hands and fell silent
as the rest. They simply turned back upstairs and put on their capes,
fetching their mother's cloak, too, which she put on over her austere black
dress.

'I'm glad our hair is fresh-washed,' whispered Sol to her sister, and
Alvar Fañez overheard and wanted to laugh. But laughter would have been
out of place.

The next he knew, Doña Jimena was standing in the doorway, a
daughter held by each hand. 'Well, Alvar Fañez? Let us not keep my
husband waiting. I am ready.' Not ten minutes had passed.

An hour or so behind Doña Jimena and Alvar Fañez, the women of the Vivar household followed along – a bright jumble of trunks and donkeys, saddlebags and bed rolls, baskets and chickens. They scowled a little into the low evening sun, and complained that they had not had time to braid their hair. But they left behind them their relations and friends, their tithed houses and all the familiar sights of Vivar, and without question were off to Valencia to serve their master and mistress. None of them expected to see home again. But not a word of misgiving passed their lips and not a word of complaint on the long, uncomfortable journey. They caught up with the Doña Jimena and bedded her down, her and the girls, on long cushions brought from the window seats of the farmhouse. And they slept wrapped in their cloaks on the hard ground. And even if they did dream of barbarous faces and murderous curved swords and a steaming red sun flaying the ground to ashes, well, they said nothing about it when they woke next morning.

Only when Valencia finally came into view did they all burst into tears at once, overcome with joy at the sight of ten thousand orange trees, the clean, pretty houses, the high, unshakeable wall and the proper sanitation. 'Whaa, mistress, but he's found you a fine place to live here,' they sniffed, and they grinned and wiped their faces and wagged their warm northern hats, and the sweat poured down their foreheads and the tears poured down their cheeks.

In front of the city gates were three strange wooden towers built of planks. They stood about the height of a battle tent, and little white flags flapped at the top. As Alvar Fañez and the party of women approached, a figure rode out of the city gate on a big chestnut horse, his lance crumpled by the heat haze that hung between them. At a frenzied gallop, he rode at the wooden towers and smashed one with a single blow of his lance. He demolished the next with his axe, and overthrew the third with a spiked and swinging mace. Then, weaving between the rubble, he executed a double figure of eight, smashing the planks to splinters and snatching up the flags that had topped the towers.

These he carried, bunched like lilies, at arm's length above his head as he galloped towards the Vivar women. Doña Jimena's horse fell back a pace or two as Babieca the mare ploughed to a halt in front of her. Wild-eyed, Don Rodrigo stared into his wife's face.

'Madam,' he said, and it seemed as if he expected at any moment to go blind, from the way he studied her face.

'Sir,' she replied, and her knuckles whitened where they clutched the pommel of her saddle. There was a silence as weighty as lead.

'What a display of arms!' said Alvar Fañez nervously loud. The waiting-women nodded enthusiastically and clapped. 'Magnificent!'

'Splendid!' 'How very gallant!' 'What chivalry!' Still Rodrigo and Jimena stared unsmiling into each other's faces.

She got down. He got down and laid the bunch of flags on the ground at her feet. The two girls, Elvira and Sol, slipped quickly out of their saddles and moved closer, taking their parents' hands to form a square.

'Six years,' said Alvar Fañez to himself, and he waved the waiting-women on into the city and followed on behind, leaving the little family standing alone on the plain of orange trees. Not one of them stole a backward glance. No one could ever boast of seeing tears in the eyes of El Cid that day. But it is said that the fruit of certain trees nearby tasted of salt that summer.

Women! The young men of El Cid's army had been fighting, besieging and marching come summer, come winter, some for as long as six years. They had seen the dark eyes of Moorish women flash hate at them over the rims of their spangled veils. But they had not seen skin nor hair of a northern woman since the exile of Don Rodrigo from Vivar. Now they strutted and pranced up and down beneath the windows of the palace in the hope that Doña Jimena's waiting-women might be watching from behind the grilles. They mended their clothes, they combed their moustaches, they groomed their beards. They daubed themselves with cloying southern scents – attar of roses and musk, and their hair shone oil-slick black.

They were not wrong. The women *were* behind the grilles. Don Rodrigo walked into the gallery next day and found them all kneeling up along the velvet benches, peering through the delicate wrought-iron. 'To the balconies, ladies!' he said, and they all squealed with surprise and overbalanced. 'To the balconies, I said! You can see better from there. Choose yourselves husbands from among my men, and to every couple married tomorrow I shall give a hundred golden crowns. The repairs to the Cathedral of Saint Estabán are complete: you may marry there. Go along now, and choose well!'

The women gave a cacophonous squeal, put their fingers to their red cheeks, then to their skirts, and ran, petticoats blooming like carnations, to the palace balconies. Doña Jimena entered silently behind her husband and slipped her hand through his arm. 'That was kind, husband.'

In these first days, it cost Don Rodrigo great effort to keep his face from the indignity of smiling. He was like a sailor in a high wind trying to stow a sail. Tatters of smile broke out here and there which he had to wrestle with before they could be hidden away. 'God's blessing on them all. They deserve everything I can give them for the loyalty they've shown you,' he said, and his eyes laughed.

On the balcony, the women were leaning over and picking husbands like fruit at a market. 'You there, with the pink cheeks!'

'No, not you, the one behind with the red beard!'

'You – yes – you, if you could just turn about so I can see you on all sides . . .'

Then one after another, they caught sight of movements beyond the city wall, among the distant orchards. A column of troops was coming – a procession that glittered in the sun like a rippling snake.

'It's the King's banner!' 'It's the King's guard!' 'And look! Look, there's the King's carriage. He's come to Valencia!' 'Somebody tell Don Rodrigo! The King Alfonso has come to Valencia himself!'

The Bridegrooms and the Palace Cat

The Infante Diego stood up in his stirrups and eased his screwed-up cloak out from under him. For days he had been in the saddle. It felt like years. He hated his brother Fernando for ever suggesting the journey. He hated King Alfonso for agreeing to the tedious trip to Valencia, even though they had gone to enormous pains to accompany him. He hated the King for riding all the way in a comfortable coach and only now exchanging it for a horse. But he caught the King's eye as Alfonso descended from his carriage, and grinned until his jaw ached and bowed low from the saddle and said jovially between teeth gritted with pain, 'How Valencia will rejoice to see you coming, my lord King. In all the excitement, I do *beg* you not to forget, in your hour of triumph, our humble suit of love.'

The King smiled back. 'I won't forget, Diego. The idea pleases me greatly.' Alfonso mounted his war horse, flicked a grain of dust off his knee and arranged the animal's mane decorously. Diego hated that round, royal bottom settling, well cushioned and unbruised, into the comfortable royal saddle.

Don Rodrigo did have time to change his clothes. But when he came out to meet his King he was wearing the simplest of linen robes, a leather belt round his hips and no piece of gold at all. No humble subject's appearance must ever outshine the King's. He dismounted from Babieca and lay face down on the ground, pressing his face so close to the earth that there were grass stains on his nose and forehead when the King urged him to his feet. Mildly embarrassed and profoundly pleased by this display, Alfonso declared, 'What's this? I had heard that "El Cid" was King of Valencia! Shall we not greet each other as equals?'

'Never!' said Don Rodrigo, dropping his head forward on to his chest. 'Every conquest I have made I made in your name and the name of God. I am your loyal subject and always will be. Take my sword. Here, take my faithful old horse. Everything I own is yours.'

The King looked over El Cid's renowned horse. It had battle scars, and tufts of its hair were missing; it had big feet and rather heavy knees. Alfonso decided he did not really want El Cid's horse. 'Don Rodrigo! Friend! Cherished as such a present would be, I could not take the war horse from under a fighting man. Mount up and show me Valencia. Show me the *Spanish* city of Valencia!'

Rodrigo heaved a silent sigh of relief as he settled once more in the saddle. His fingers knotted in the mane of his beloved horse. He had determined to give the King whatsoever he desired. But he was very glad Alfonso did not want Babieca.

Riding past the flowery terraces and wrought-iron filigree of the city, King Alfonso determined not to ask for anything from Don Rodrigo. It was important to tread warily. El Cid commanded more men than in all the divisions of Castile put together. He had conquered an area greater than the King's entire kingdom. If he chose to, El Cid could be a dangerous enemy. Alfonso's heart pattered and quaked with relief to find that Rodrigo was still a loyal subject and not a warlord with ambitions to be a king. No, he would ask for nothing from the treasures of Valencia. Instead, he would pay El Cid the greatest diplomatic compliment he could think of.

'Don Rodrigo Díaz, your daughters are as lovely as two fantail pigeons,' he said as the girls curtsied to him amidst the gleaming tiled walls of the banqueting hall. 'Castile is darker now by the loss of three candles: your excellent wife and the exquisite Sol and Emelda.' (Elvira looked up and was about to correct him when her mother frowned a discouraging frown.) 'In fact two young men were so desolated with grief by their departure that they came to Us with tears on their cheeks and begged to accompany Us on this journey. Two young men of noble birth, yet not so proud that they must look for royal brides. Their love has lighted on your two daughters, Don Rodrigo, and it is my joy to permit the marriage. Sol! Emelda! I give you the Infantes Diego and Fernando!'

The King flourished one arm towards the door, and Diego stumbled into the room, pushed from behind by his brother. The two of them bared their teeth in massive smiles, and bowed so deeply that their jacket tails flopped up their backs. Sol and Elvira clutched each other's hands and, if their mother had not signalled them to curtsy, they might have twirled each other round in a dance.

Delighted with himself, King Alfonso turned to accept Don Rodrigo's thanks . . . and found himself looking at a face ashen with fury. His back rigid, his beard trembling slightly and his tight-shut mouth invisible behind it, Rodrigo appeared to grow in stature, to swell up, to darken like a storm cloud. The King's heart pattered away to shelter somewhere behind his backbone. El Cid was *not* pleased.

'They're too young,' he said at last.

'Nonsense,' said the King with a squeak of laughter.

'They're *too young*!'

Suddenly the blood swarmed behind Alfonso's eyes. His old prejudices came flooding back. He could see it all now: all that old arrogance, all that bolt-upright priggish superiority. His present was spoiled. Rodrigo had snubbed his generosity. The noble Infantes were *not good enough* for the daughters of this peasant-born jackanape! 'Are you refusing Our beneficence?' enquired the King, grinding his teeth as he smiled.

The Infantes stared. The Doña Jimena stared. The girls clutched each other close and held their breath.

Like a tree momentarily defying the axeman, El Cid's pride briefly towered over the King. For six years not man nor beast nor city had gainsaid him. Then, with a supreme effort, he recovered his voice: 'If the Infantes alone wanted to do me this kindness, I would refuse them. But since the honour comes from you, my King and master, I humbly and thankfully accept. The honour it bestows on my family is almost too great to bear for a mere farmer from Vivar.'

'Quite,' said the King, through clenched teeth.

Sol and Elvira danced; their mother breathed out heavily. The Infantes shook hands with one another and Fernando muttered, 'By the way, which one are you having?'

The news of the marriage spilled out of the palace and through the streets, where the waiting-women and their chosen husbands were already dancing to the music Martin the Miller played on a nasal, squawking flute. Abbot Pedro threw open the newly hung doors of the Cathedral Saint Estabán. The mother and father of the brides were swept along in the procession that swirled towards the cathedral. On the way, Doña Jimena took her husband's arm and shook it. 'What were you thinking of, Don Rodrigo? Such a match for our daughters, and you object!'

Rodrigo shook his head. 'I'm sorry. I don't know what madness took hold of me. It was as though there was a hand on my throat forbidding me to consent. But it's true. It is a wonderful match.'

Beneath a clamour of bells and a panic of seagulls, Elvira and Sol were married to the Infantes Fernando and Diego. The girls gave away their hearts and hands – and, of course, every clasp and pin, every coin and jewel, every brooch and buckle they owned into the possession of their husbands. To tell the truth, there was nothing they wanted to keep back. To tell the truth, there was no need to think of property, for the Infantes could live in Valencia for three lifetimes and not need to spend a brass halfpenny simply because they were the sons-in-law of El Cid.

On the third day after the wedding, the King Alfonso took his leave. He rode north with all his courtiers (except the two Infantes), but the wedding feast continued on for five more days. The fragrance of oranges blew in at the open doors and windows of the airy Moorish palace and wafted the smell of roasting meat and boiling vegetables far beyond the bounds of the city.

Now the siddi who had held Valencia during nine months of siege had made his escape, in a private barge, the day before the city's surrender. No trace remained of him but a scattering of belongings and his heraldic device – a lion's head – snarling in stone on every street corner, staircase and cornice. There were stone lions in the gardens and bronze lions on the roofs. There were lions in the tapestries and lead-lipped lions spewed water out of their mouths at the public drinking fountains. The feet of the chairs were like lion's paws, and the arms of the siddi's throne were carved with lion masks. What no one had realized was that the escaping siddi, hurrying away secretly by night with as much treasure as he could muster, had left behind his pet, his mascot, his living, breathing heraldic device – a lion.

The beast sloped away from all the confused noises and smells of the invasion and hid itself in the attic rooms of the palace, eating the hide off the couches stored there, whenever hunger rumbled. But the smell of the wedding feast summoned the lion like a gong. It roamed about the palace, pushing its nose in at every door, clearing whole tables of the remnants of meat, clattering goblets of wine, lapping the juices off silver salvers. If anyone saw it, they were too swayed by drink to believe their eyes, and it was not until the beast reached the central banqueting hall that the alarm was raised.

Couched on sofas of zebra-skin, the most important guests were reclining around a low table of half-eaten delights. There was not one fully awake. The gaunt and sober Don Rodrigo, seated in the siddi's stiff-backed chair, had long since tired of eating and closed his eyes so as to think. Thought had turned to sleep, and his big head had fallen forwards on his chest. The bridegrooms too were asleep on their backs, all snores and sprawls. The women, talking quietly with their heads close together, had also nodded off to sleep.

The lion pushed the door open with one paw and padded in. It lapped up the wine out of the cup which dangled from Fernando's sleeping hand and its tongue explored Fernando's fingers.

'Uh? Who's that? Erch! What the devil . . .?' The lion looked at Fernando; Fernando looked into the lion's yellow eyes. He rolled backwards off his couch and made frantic swimming motions to drag himself across the marble floor. A chest of linen – a wedding gift from the King – stood open by the wall. Fernando heaved out a pile of sheets and rolled inside, pulling the lid shut with a bang which woke Diego.

When Diego saw the lion, he stood up on his couch, his knees knocking, and pointed at the women: at Doñas Jimena, Sol, and Elvira. His voice croaked soundlessly, 'Eat them, not me! Nice tender women! Yum-yum! Eat them! Oh, Mother of God save me and I'll build a cathedral in your honour right here in Valencia! Oh, Alvar Fañez! Dear, darling Alvar, kill it for me! Chop it in pieces! Oh God, save me! I'm too young to die!'

The lion blinked up at him, its ears flickering. Diego shut his eyes and leapt into the folds of the curtains and climbed up to the pelmet, tucking his feet up by his hands. The women stirred, but could not see the lion at first as it was hidden from them by the table. It padded softly between the lion-claw feet of a couch, and rested its jaw on the pair of feet below the throne – where the siddi had always sat. Alvar Fañez got silently, slowly to his feet, searching about for a sword: no one at the wedding was armed. Bishop Pedro and Don Bermúdez were also on their feet, watching, with horror written on their faces.

Tickled awake, Don Rodrigo looked down and saw the lion licking his shins. The animal was disconcerted by the change of smell: not the smooth, black skin of the siddi but wiry-haired white legs: not a Moorish but a Christian smell. Piqued, the lion drew its velvet lips back off its yellow teeth and snarled.

'Get away with you, you stupid beast,' said Rodrigo softly, and he plunged both hands into its mane. He wrestled it over on its back and combed its stomach and chest-mane with his fingers, sending up clouds of attic dust which made them both sneeze. The lion wagged its legs in the air and its paws clambered about El Cid's arms. But the claws were sheathed now, and a deep purr rumbled through the room like distant thunder.

'You ladies,' he said, without looking up. 'Kindly find a safer place until I have disposed of this fellow . . . Slowly, now. Move very slowly.' The ladies withdrew.

At length, Rodrigo rolled the animal on its feet and taking it by the scruff of its mane walked it firmly out of doors to lock it in an empty stable. He never once took his eyes off the lion's head. So he did not see

Diego clinging to the curtain rod, nor Fernando peeping out of the chest.

When the Conqueror was gone from the banqueting room, Alvar Fañez went to the chest and opened the lid. 'You can get out now, your lordship. And you, noble Infante, you can come down from the ceiling.'

Bishop Pedro began to laugh uncontrollably with relief, clutching his overfull stomach and pointing at Diego as he slid down the curtains. Alvar Fañez was tempted to smile as well, but Fernando, shouldering him out of the way as he stalked out of the room, said shrilly, 'Well, *you* didn't do a lot either, did you? Yes – priest – hold your tongue if you don't want it cut out some dark night.'

'Insolent young puppy,' said Bermudez, staring after him. But Alvar Fañez caught him by the shoulder and stopped him.

'He's right. We didn't do much either. And if you take my advice we'll keep quiet about this.'

'Why?' exclaimed Bishop Pedro. 'I'd like to put a smile on the face of El Cid: he's too solemn by half. Wait till I tell him how it went! He didn't see them!'

Alvar Fañez put his fingers to his lips and said softly, 'Don Rodrigo can just – *just*, I say – overlook the fact that his sons-in-law are graceless fops and dandies with melons for brains. Please don't ask him to accept that they are cowards, too. Believe me, it wouldn't bring a smile to his face. I think it might even break his heart.'

At that moment, Don Rodrigo put his head round the door. 'Is everybody well? Nobody eaten? The ladies were not unsettled, I hope.'

'I'll go right away and put their minds at rest,' said the good Bishop.

El Cid's eyes gleamed with pleasure after the excitement. 'Poor old beast. Forgotten and left behind. What a shame my sons-in-law weren't here to see it. What a chance they missed for a trial of arms on their wedding day! What a tribute they could have made of its capture to Sol and Elvira!' Don Bermúdez and Alvar Fañez looked back at him with blank, silent faces, then put on smiles and nodded enthusiastically. 'No matter. They'll have plenty of opportunity to prove themselves tomorrow. Break the news gently to the ladies, Bishop Pedro, I beg you.'

'What news?'

'About the army of King Mu'taman,' said Don Rodrigo with an unlaughing delight. 'Didn't you know? It's encamped round the city walls. Even now, we are under siege. Fifty thousand men. I thank God for the

honour He has done me in sending this challenge! Don't you, Bishop?'

The Bishop sat down sharply and coughed. 'Er . . . yes . . .well, yes I suppose so.' El Cid hurried away. There were a great many preparations to be made if he was to break the siege.

'El Cid and the King of Morocco. This will be the battle to end all battles,' said Don Bermúdez solemnly. 'Fifty thousand men, did he say?'

'The more the enemy, the greater the glory,' said Alvar Fañez almost automatically. Laying a hand on Bermúdez' sleeve he added, 'Find the Infantes, will you, and bring them to me? We have certain *details of battle* to discuss, if El Cid's heart is to be kept from breaking.'

'Them? They won't come out of the closet till it's all over,' said Bermúdez disgustedly, and spat on the floor.

'Oh, my noble friend, believe me. If I have my way, the Infantes will come out of this battle with more glory than El Cid himself.'

'You're a good man, Alvar Fañez.'

'We serve according to our skills,' he replied vaguely. His eyes were on the bent and sagging curtain rail, and the spilled chest of linen.

Cowardly Heroes

'In all my life I've never been so afraid as this,' said Sol to her sister, though she made very sure that her mother and father did not hear. From the battlements of Valencia, they could see the tents of the King of Morocco's army patterning the plain like a carpet, with circles of dark brocade and fringes of white rope. In the bay, sails moved across the water like the crests of breaking waves and spilled Moors ashore as numberless and relentless as the pebbles rolled by a tide. The King Mu'taman's tent, horned and scarlet as the Devil, lapped the ground with pennant banners of silver and gold.

'That tent is mine,' said Don Rodrigo. 'I shall take it myself – and the man inside it. I leave any other winnings to you, men. Doña Jimena, I thank God from the bottom of my heart for this chance to prove my mettle before your eyes. I daresay you said to yourself often, these past years, "That husband of mine has an easy life!"'

'Oh, often, often,' said Jimena drily, but her knuckles were white where she gripped the stone parapet.

'I have a favour to ask, Commander,' said Alvar Fañez.

'Anything old friend.'

'Give me your valiant sons-in-law to fight at my left and right hand, and I will carve a swath through the flank of Mu'taman's army. Their skill as riders and swordsmen is famed throughout the earth.'

'Is it? Is it really? Oh, yes, yes. Excellent.' A glow of pleasure lit Rodrigo's eyes, and he did not notice the look of astonishment on the faces of his daughters – no such rumour had reached *them*.

Alvar Fañez hurried to the palace. It did not take him long to find Fernando and Diego hiding under their beds and whimpering. He hauled them out by their heels. 'Get on your armour. It falls to me to make heroes out of you, and I hate to fail in any task. I don't mean to fail. So call horses and then do exactly what I tell you . . .'

He manhandled them on to the tallest, heaviest horses, and fastened long lunge reins to the cheekbands of each bridle. Don Bermúdez rode on their left and Martin the Miller on their right. Fañez crimped their stirrups so tight around their armoured feet that they could not dismount, and he trotted them smartly round to the east gate of the city, where they would be out of sight of Don Rodrigo.

Into the silence which precedes every battle, the voice of King Mu'taman's heralds rose like Muslim prayers: 'Come down, the man who calls himself El Siddi! You who serve him, give him up. Give up Valencia into the hands that beautified it and to Allah who protects it. Rodrigo Díaz de Vivar – spare the lives of your children and womenfolk. Come out and offer up your throat for the cutting!'

Rodrigo answered in person, though he did not strain to shout: 'I did not give myself the name El Siddi. It came from the lips of Muslim men. And I care not whether I conquer today with the name of Díaz, Cid or Conqueror, for I conquer in the name of God!' He called to Bishop Pedro, who was standing at the top of the cathedral steps, 'Bless our men, my friend, and let's be about the day's work!'

With some grunting and groaning, Bishop Pedro lifted into the air a massy gold cross, and bellowed in rich Barcelona Spanish: 'The bliss of

eternal life for every man who dies today . . . and a sackful of Moorish gold for every man who doesn't. Now let me at them!' He dropped the cross into the outstretched arms of his altar boys, threw off his cope and cape (showing himself to be in full armour) and waddled down the steps on to the rump of a huge war horse. If the guard had not opened the front gates, he would have ridden straight through them, and he was first on to the field in the battle to end all battles.

The Moors threw down the tent poles of their battle tents: all but the King's own horned and scarlet pavilion billowed to the grass. Arrows splintered through the air as the sea splinters sunlight. Strange Moorish chariots hurtled like comets. Hooves crushed a million oranges until the earth was a quagmire of juice. And souls were plucked from their owners as readily as the oranges from a tree, and men kissed their shadows on the green ground and died.

Towing the Infantes behind him, Alvar Fañez carved out a path through the Moorish troops just as he had promised. He cut down those who came at him from front or sides, and Bermúdez and Martín protected his back as well as the shrieking, squealing Infantes. Two, three, four times the knot of horses raked the field as a comb rakes lice from a head of hair. But increasingly, the Moors came by with their swords across their backs, bent forward over their horses' necks and with their eyes unfocussed by fear. 'Allah is in his arm!' they yelled.

'No! No! A demon, not Allah!'

'El Siddi is not a man! El Siddi is a demon!'

'There is no killing him! He will live for ever!'

In the thickest part of the mêlée, Don Rodrigo, mounted on Babieca and wielding the silver sword called Colada, winnowed the Moors, and their souls flew up like husks off a winnowing floor. Those who stood between him and the tent of Mu'taman fell like corn under the scythe. They clawed for their swords, they levelled their lances or they dived in panic out of their saddles, but it made no difference. El Cid rode through them as a shark splits the water with its fins, its eyes fastened on the meat ahead.

Out from behind the tent sprang King Mu'taman himself, on a rearing, leaping horse. He set his lance at Rodrigo's heart . . . and saw it splintered by his sword. The flakes of rich red paint spattered Babieca's mane like blood, but El Cid was unhurt. Shoulder to shoulder the horses met, knee to knee the riders; their thighs jarred within their hips. As the King drew out his sword, Rodrigo grasped its curved blade in both mailed

hands and threw it aside. Mu'taman snatched at Rodrigo's beard, and their eyes met and their foreheads clashed.

'I am stronger,' rasped Rodrigo, jarring the King backwards into his saddle.

'And I am younger,' replied Mu'taman as he turned his horse's head away. 'Time is with me, El Siddi!'

'And God with me!'

A furious chase began. But Babieca was weary already from fighting her way through the sea of Moors. King Mu'taman escaped the field, and when they saw him go, his troops went after him – all those who had not already fled.

El Cid rode back to the royal tent, and there Babieca recovered her wind and the generals of the Christian army mustered to the flag of Valencia.

Hidden in the shade of the orange groves, Alvar Fañez cut off the lunging reins and prised the stirrups lose from the Infantes' armoured feet. He put his own bloody sword into Fernando's hand, his lance into Diego's. They were late arriving at the mustering point.

'You're not hurt: I'm very pleased to see it!' exclaimed Don Rodrigo peering into the faces of his sons-in-law. They seemed to be weary past speech. Alvar Fañez had to speak for them.

'Oh, master! I can barely find words to describe the battle your noble sons-in-law fought! See how the noble Diego's sword is red to the hilt. See how the valiant Fernando's lance is repainted with the blood of the Moors! Each time I went to engage an enemy, the Infantes were there before me. Don Bermúdez can bear witness: he saw us on the field. Friend Martin will never be done telling the credit they were to their father-in-law today!'

'Is this true?' Don Rodrigo slipped Babieca between the Infantes' horses and clasped the boys' heads against his shoulders. He was very close to tears. 'You are a pride and a joy to me, my sons. I humbly admit that until now I misjudged you for spoiled darlings with water in your blood. But you are past praise. You're past the deserving of anything I can give you. I've already given you the most precious things I own – I mean Sol and Elvira. But whatever you desire from the spoils of this victory, name it and it shall be yours. Whatever you covet from Valencia – from the gold on the domes to the flowers in the ground – it's all yours for the taking!' (Fernando and Diego showed signs of recovering; they stirred cheerfully in their saddles.) 'Heroes in battle! Do you hear that, Bishop Pedro? You must write to your old master, Count Ramón, and tell him that El Cid is

outstripped by two far greater knights – his own sons! Didn't you hear the brave words of Alvar Fañez?'

The Bishop was sweaty, battle-soiled and weary. 'I heard them. I heard them or I would have said such heroes were the inventions of a story-teller or a liar.' Alvar Fañez kicked him in the ankle, and then the Bishop knew that he had guessed rightly. 'But Alvar Fañez is a good man, so I believe every word he speaks. Indeed, he is a very good man,' and he made a small, secret gesture of blessing Fañez.

El Cid threw off his chain-mail hood so that his linen coif fell creased on to his shoulders, and he put back his head and laughed out loud for sheer joy.

'Yes, indeed,' said Bishop Pedro. 'You are a very good man, Alvar Fañez.'

'Heroes, eh?' said Fernando lowering himself into a chair in the corner of the room. He searched about for somewhere to rest his feet, and laid them on the holy shrine where Elvira said her prayers each morning.

Diego had not yet stopped trembling. 'I was petrified! I'll get that Alvar Fañez if it's the last thing I do! That peasant tried to get us both killed! I've lost my voice with screaming. I can't stop my teeth chattering.'

'Stop whining,' said his brother peeling an orange and throwing the rind at Diego. 'It paid off, didn't it? We can take what we like, and believe me, I can think of a thing or two to take.'

'As far as I'm concerned, you can keep it. I hate this place,' said Diego, squatting down in the angle of the wall, gibbering, and clapping his arms with his hands. 'Lions roaming about, uncouth common soldiers sitting down at dinner with us, the Doña Jimena praying every minute of the day, and nowhere to buy a decent jacket. That Fañez is laughing behind his hand at us – he has been ever since the business with the lion. There are Moors crawling out of the knotholes: Moors climbing up the walls. There's even Moors fighting in the Bastard's own army! This is no place to live. I don't know why I ever let you talk me into this. I hate the South. I hate Valencia!'

'Shut your noise,' said Fernando, throwing the whole orange at his brother. 'Who needs to stay?'

'What?'

'Well, I ask you? What could we ask for today that Papa Bastard would refuse? So I say we ask to take our holy little wives and go north again, where we belong.'

Diego stopped shivering and stood up. 'That's genius, Fernando.

That's absolute, devil-clever genius, you son of a . . . Can we take plenty of money with us?'

'All we can carry, and all the carts in Valencia to carry it in. We'll leave this place looking like an egg the day before Easter. Now, shall I talk to Papa Bastard or will you?' He smirked at his brother's squirming joy.

'You! You do it,' said Diego with little jerking thrusts of his hands. 'Go on. You do it. You're older than me.'

'Go?' Don Rodrigo's voice echoed in the vaulted roof of the room. The Doña Jimena's hand leapt to her rosary.

'Go?'

'Indeed, yes,' said Fernando, quickly rising off one knee. 'This city is the crown and glory of El Cid, the Conqueror. And three heads can never wear a single crown. It is time for my brother and I to carve out triumphs of our own – to found new houses out of the blood line of El Cid, so that our triple fame will one day hold up the three corners of the sky!'

'Oh, yes, I do understand.' Rodrigo was anxious not to give offence. 'But so soon! I've been parted from little Sol and Elvira for so long, and now, after just a week . . . Forgive me, Fernando, I mustn't stand in your way. If you feel you have to go, then of course you must. All my joy rests in knowing that my daughters have found good husbands who will look after them – make them proud . . .'

'My dear father, my heart cracks at the thought of leaving you and the saintly Doña Jimena and all those charming rustic officers of yours. But our destiny cries out. Both Diego and I have had dreams . . . extraordinary dreams . . .'

'Then I would be standing in the way of God Himself if I were to stop you going,' said Don Rodrigo, winning the struggle within himself. He glanced at his wife, and she lowered her dark-lashed eyes and said, 'They have had dreams. Clearly it is meant to be.'

Diego procured four carts and four Moorish slaves to drive them. He and his brother loaded the carts with everything that took their fancy: statues, feather beds, draperies, caskets and crates of jewellery and coin. They even took the golden altar rail – 'We shall found a new church one day soon, in thanksgiving for our fortunate marriages' – from Saint Estabán Cathedral.

Little Sol and Elvira saw nothing of these preparations. They were pouring out their tears into the laps of their mother and father, and making their farewells. Journeys were not so common nor lives so long in those days that kin who parted company could be sure of meeting again.

'While King Mu'taman lives, I must not leave Valencia unprotected, or I would ride with you part of the way,' said Don Rodrigo, gnawing at his beard.

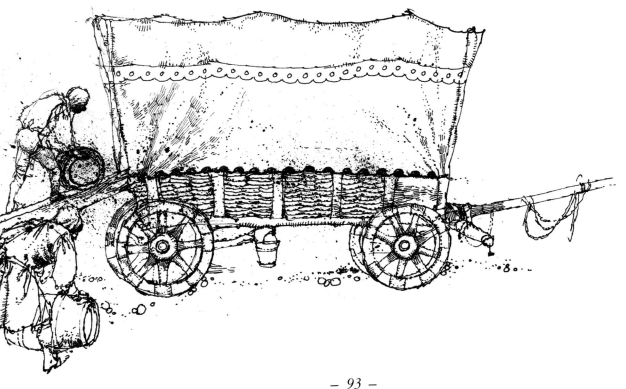

'We have two heroes to protect us, father,' replied Elvira bravely.

But when Rodrigo saw the four carts loaded to mountainous peaks with glittering valuables, he could not help bursting out, 'My dear sons! Let me send a troop of horsemen with you to protect you and your belongings. There are bandits hereabouts!'

Diego shot an uneasy glance at Fernando, who merely grasped his lapels grandly and asked, 'Father! Do you not trust us to protect our own?'

Bishop Pedro came out of his palace, rubbing his hands together with a breezy cheerfulness. 'But you'll let me come along, won't you?' he said.

'*No!*' said both brothers emphatically.

'What? Not to say mass and offer up prayers to God night and morning?'

'Yes, yes, do come!' cried the girls.

'Yes, grant me that one favour,' said Don Rodrigo. And the Infantes, seeing no way round it, said, 'Of course! Why, the good Bishop does us honour by his kind suggestion!'

'What's his game?' muttered Diego uneasily, as the Infantes mounted up.

'How should I know?' snapped Fernando.

Two days out from Valencia, the Bishop Pedro began to scold himself. 'You silly old man, Pedro,' he muttered crossly. 'What are you doing here? What uncharitable, suspicious thoughts brought you trailing after these noble young gentlemen, putting yourself to all this discomfort, leaving behind your warm bed in Valencia? So they're cowards in battle; there are worse things than cowardice! And the young ladies are clearly in love with them. The Infantes weren't raised as soldiers: they're not to blame if they are cowards. And if they find themselves some quiet place to live, and do their duty to God and their wives, then what's wrong with that?'

At midday he happened to ask of Diego, 'And which way do we turn beyond the forest?'

'What business is it of yours?' snapped Diego.

Fernando glared at his brother. 'As fate leads, señor.'

'But you're not heading back to Castile?'

'What if we are?' raged Diego.

'Ah, now, Bishop Pedro, where would we find glory and adventure by simply going back to the comforts of León?' said Fernando with a condescending smile. 'But I'll tell you what, dear friend. I do believe it's time for you to be turning back.'

'Oh, I don't mind. I'll come a little further.'

'Go back.'

'But I . . .'

'Go back, damn you! Leave us alone, you conniving old woman!' (When Fernando lost his temper it was viler by far than Diego's.) 'I don't know what you think to gain by traipsing around behind us. I don't know what trick you think you're working or what favour you're chasing, but there's no employment for fat old priests with us! So get back to the other peasants in Valencia. Your low birth won't be noticed there, for there's none of higher degree than the scullery boys. Pssss. Go on. Get back to El Bastard.'

Shoulder to shoulder, they watched Bishop Pedro weave his way back through the trees casting anxious backward glances at the startled girl-brides. The carts were moving: they could not jump down. And they were too far off to have heard the sharp exchange of words. But they called his name and waved their hands as if to fetch him back.

'He'll go whining to Rodrigo,' whispered Diego.

'He's a foreigner. Trusting Papa won't believe his word against the word of Alvar Fañez, and that peasant is determined El Cid should think we're the best fellows in the world. I can't imagine why. Some plot, I suppose. Come on. A mile or two more and we can shed some of our *unnecessary baggage*.'

'What can you mean?' Diego giggled, wiping his nose on his glove.

The carts and the string of horses clanged and jostled their way between the trees, until night noises began to murmur. At dusk they were still moving through the forest of Corpes. Fernando told the slaves to make camp, and then gave Diego an encouraging wink. Both bridegrooms lifted their brides down from the carts with great gentleness, and led them away from the camp clearing:

'Let's walk a little while dinner is prepared.'

'Come my darling and let's talk of love where only the trees can hear us.'

'Why did you send Bishop Pedro away?' asked Elvira, as she had been longing to do all day. But Fernando did not answer.

The camp fire was nothing but a glitter through the trees now. The stars above the branch tops were brighter by far.

'Aren't you afraid of the wolves and wild beasts?' asked Sol, pressing close against her husband. But Diego did not answer. The two couples were just within sight of each other – pale shapes between the dark trunks. Diego suddenly called out to his brother through the darkness, 'I don't think I can use a sword to do it!'

'No matter,' replied Fernando. 'Besides, the blade would spoil the dress. Don't forget the dress.' His voice was sharp like an icicle. He cupped Elvira's chin in one hand, then raised his other fist and smashed it down into the white oval of Elvira's starlit face. Leaning her against a tree, he followed up the blow with several more to her body.

'My love! What have I done? Tell me what I've done! Ah!' As she fell among the dark roots, night creatures scuttered among the leaf mould, and Fernando kicked with the side of his foot – kicked and kicked and kicked again. His fingers, fumbling for the laces of her dress, met with her fingers instead, but he flung her hands aside and wrested off her velvet dress. Then he took off his belt and set about beating the life out of his little wife.

He found his brother in the dark by listening for the cries of Sol. But by the time he reached him, there was silence, and Diego was rolling Sol's stolen dress into a clumsy bundle. A white shape lay smudged into the leaf-mould. Diego stood up, rebuckling his belt. 'It was easy,' he said proudly.

'At last we're rid of them,' said Fernando. 'Their low birth clung to me like manure.' And he shuddered at the remembered dishonour of marrying with a *farmer's daughter*.

A wolf howled, and Bishop Pedro felt a shiver like death run down his spine. He turned his horse . . . then turned it again, set its head for Valencia, then reined it in. An unseen hand seemed to be tugging on his shoulder, telling him to turn back.

'They're not fit to wait table on the daughters of El Cid,' he said aloud. And then he whispered to himself, 'Just because they insulted you. Weren't they right, you simpleton? You *are* an old woman.' He rode a little farther south.

'Yes, but they're foul-mouthed and shameless! They have no respect for their father-in-law: they call him El . . . They have no respect. And if they have no respect for him, what are their true feelings for the girls?' He set his spurs to his horse and galloped blindly back into the forest, the unlit branches snatching at his head and shoulders, the twigs clawing at his back.

With no way of seeing the correct path, he let instinct guide him, and he prayed as he rode: 'God forgive me if I'm too late!' Through the trees he could see the grey shape of wolves skulking in packs, and the flicker of green eyes, and the occasional growling roar warned of bigger beasts scavenging the forests for food.

Something made him stop and listen – to the wild animals, his horse's strained breathing, the creaking of the boughs overhead. And then he heard it – the spit of a dying fire. He followed the smell of the smoke, and found the Infantes' camp fire, lit and at once abandoned. The carts had moved on into the night, and on the edge of the clearing, as round and pale as the white capped mushrooms that were sprouting among the tree roots, was the face of Elvira Díaz.

She had dragged herself towards the glimmer of the dying fire. Her sister was still curled unconscious a little farther on. The Bishop wrapped one in his cloak, the other in his coat. He fanned the fire into life, and fed it to keep the wolves away. 'A big grey one sniffed at me,' said Sol, 'but I said my prayers and it went away.' Elvira's eyes were empty and dull as she lay beside the fire. Nothing but the tenderness of Pedro's nursing kept her alive through the night.

By first light, he sat them on his horse and led them painfully, painstakingly out of the forest and south. For a whole day Elvira did not speak at all, though the Bishop would lift her battered face and turn it towards the sun and say, 'Soon you will be home with your mother and father. Soon you will be home.'

Then one time she pushed his hand away and said, through swollen lips, 'You do me no kindness, señor. You should have left us to the wolves. We are shamed everlastingly. Shamed.' And a shiver ran through the trees, that boded rain.

'Shamed!' cried the King Mu'taman, and the sand dunes of Morocco shivered and spilled their crests into the valleys. 'Allah must be revenged!'

'Shamed!' cried El Cid, as he lifted his daughters down in the courtyard of Valencia's palace.

'The shame is all mine,' said Alvar Fañez, running from the palace. 'I deceived you into believing the Infantes were heroes and men. I lied! I wanted to make you happy! I lied so that you shouldn't be saddened by the truth! I knew the truth – and now your daughters, whom I love like the little angels in heaven, have paid the price of my foolishness.'

Alvar Fañez felt better when he had made his confession. But Don Rodrigo had not heard one word of it. He carried each girl to her bed in his own arms, then went to his own rooms and shut the door against Alvar Fañez, against Bishop Pedro, against Doña Jimena herself.

'Shamed!' whispered the Moorish slaves among themselves, as they entered Castile driving the Infantes' cartloads of treasure. 'We have left the service of El Siddi, the Conqueror, to cower at the heels of two murderous dogs. Shame on our mothers that we were ever born to such dishonour.' But Diego and Fernando were within sight of home, and their blue blood pumped a little faster at the thought of returning to civilization twice as rich as when they left, and at last free from shame.

The Revenge of El Cid

'El Cid is coming!'
    'El Cid of Valencia!'
    'El Cid and a column of men!'
    'El Cid with carriages and horses!'
    'El Cid is on the square!'

'I have heard of this El Cid,' said the Prince of Navarre to the Prince of Aragón. 'I have a mind to see him.'

King Alfonso struggled with the small fastenings at the collar of his robe and stumbled on the hem. 'Why now, with the Princes here on state visit?' He sent for his marshal-at-arms and he sent for his chancellor. He sent for his body-guard too, as he ran the length of the draughty corridor in unbuckled shoes. At the top of the stairs he caught his breath and patted down his hair. At the foot of the stairs he collected himself and centred his belt buckle over his stomach. Settling into his throne, he hid his feet under his robe and breathed deeply twice. 'We grant audience to Don Rodrigo Díaz. Let him enter.'

The double doors swung open and into the audience chamber came a figure more grand, more impressive than any of the worthy noblemen whose portraits panelled the wall. Don Rodrigo wore boots of liquorice-dark leather cuffed and double-cuffed above the knee. His undershirt spilled foaming lace at his throat and cuffs, and over it he wore a doublet of blood-red velvet and sleeves of white calf suede, with silver embroidery along the long-lapped collar. A cuirass of chased gold arched over his sternum, and his hips were girded round with a leather belt a hand's width wide. His white kid breeches still carried the red stains of his saddle, and gold spurs clanged against the floor: their spinning ferrule wheels mesmerized the onlookers who crowded in from all quarters of the palace. His hair was a mane of grey and sunbleached gold, and his beard, which reached now as far as his belt, was looped round with a white lanyard according to the custom of noblemen. His big hands were mailed in silver. But where the silver sword, Colada, should have hung, there was only an empty scabbard of red Moroccan leather which just dragged along the floor.

Behind him, in robes of darkest blue, their faces and unbraided hair covered with veils of white lawn, stood Elvira and Sol. Between them, veiled in black, stood their mother. A silence thicker than wool stuffed up the open mouths of the courtiers.

Alfonso felt the old dislike and resentment stir. He felt threatened. No one should dress to outshine his King. Was this the humble subject who had lain down and rubbed his face in the grass? 'Rodrigo Díaz!' he exclaimed fulsomely. 'We had not thought to see your face again so soon. We are indeed fortunate!'

'There is bunting in the streets – and musicians on the steps. León is celebrating, I see. For the return of the Royal Infantes, no doubt.'

'Who? No, no. The Princes of Aragón and Navarre,' said the King proudly. 'What's this about the Infantes? Aren't they with you? Have you mislaid them? So careless, dear Rodrigo, ha, ha!' The King gave an embarrassed laugh and whispered under his breath to his chancellor, 'Are the Infantes here? Why? Why didn't somebody tell me?'

'I mentioned it this morning, Sire. Perhaps your thoughts were taken up with the state visit. Shall I send for them?'

There was no need. The Infantes quickly caught wind of El Cid's arrival. Fear and horrid fascination drew them helplessly towards the palace.

'I thought you said he wouldn't come here. You said he wouldn't find out!' complained Diego shrilly. 'You said the beasts would eat up the flesh and bone. And besides, you said he wouldn't leave Valencia unguarded!'

'Well, I can be wrong, can't I?' retorted Fernando. 'Trust me. Uncle Ordoñez will defend us, you'll see. There are plenty of right-thinking noblemen here in León who'll clap us on the back and praise us for what we did. You'll see.'

The empty scabbard scraped across the floor as El Cid advanced down the room.

The King asked quickly. 'And what brings you out of Valencia and all this way to León?'

A door to the rear of the King's throne squeaked on its hinges as the two Infantes crept clumsily in. The great swords called Tizan and Colada hampered them. Their eyes bulged slightly, and their cheeks were pink. El Cid raised a mailed hand and seemed about to point at them when his gesture became a simple wave of the hand.

'A mere misunderstanding, Sire, scarcely more. You may have heard how a great battle was fought for Valencia after you left. Such esteem fell to the noble Infantes, my daughters' husbands, that I bade them take for themselves anything their hearts desired. Shortly afterwards, they chose to leave Valencia. Their marriage with my daughters did not please them, it seems. But no matter . . . I regret, I should have made myself more clear. I had not thought they would choose to take with them the swords, Tizan and Colada, which were given to me as presents of surrender. I ask merely that these swords be returned to me.'

Fernando and Diego already had the swords half out of their sheaths.
'Of course!'
'Naturally!'
'How regrettable . . .'
'. . . a misunderstanding!'

Colada slipped into the scabbard at Rodrigo's side with a sigh of escaping air. By the time the hanger clanged home, Fernando and Diego were tip-toeing out of the room.

'One moment, señors!' Rodrigo called after them. 'One other *small* matter!'

They froze, shoulders hunched round their ears. Rodrigo addressed the King (which was only correct). 'When the noble Infantes left Valencia, they took with them not only my swords but some thirty thousand marks in gold and silver. Although I have already overstepped good manners by asking for the return of my swords, I find that my soldiers eat so heartily and my horses wear out their tack so disgracefully and my household makes such a squandering on clothes, that my exchequer is almost empty. Heaven forbid that I should ask for the return of my thirty thousand marks. But perhaps a loan . . .?'

'It's sent for! Consider it sent for!' gasped Diego. 'In fact I'll go and get it myself, immediately – won't we, Fernando?'

He had his fingers on the doorknob, and Fernando close on his heels, before Rodrigo spoke again. 'One word more, pray, before the Infantes rob us of their company!' And the King held up his fingers, to detain Fernando and Diego. 'The noble Infantes took more than my swords and my thirty thousand marks. They also took my daughters, their wives.' Like the red-tasselled grasses that suddenly lift their heads and shake free their seed in a burning wind, El Cid seemed to grow in stature. His voice, like his breast and mailed fist, seemed to be all metal – faster and faster, louder and louder. 'They took the Doña Sol and the Doña Elvira, and halfway here, in forest teeming with wild beasts, they stripped my daughters and beat them with belt and spur, and left them for dead. And for this I seek their blood on the ground, nor will I leave here with one drop less than I seek! My daughters are scarred in body and heart. King Alfonso of Spain, I lay their cause at your feet!'

Alfonso drew in his feet under his gown and his hands into his sleeves. 'Is this true?' A chaos of outraged voices ran deafening round the room. Only the King's advisers were dumb. 'Won't somebody speak? *Is this true?*'

'Yes, I shall speak! I shall tell the truth!' It was the Count Ordoñez. He pushed his way through from the rear of the hall, his purple and black robe and turban swathed and knotted about him like furious blood vessels. 'My nephews have told me about these *brides* of theirs, your Majesty. Oh why did I ever consent to that marriage! I should have known that the seed of a nettle will grow to nothing but rank weed. Gentlemen! Don't be deceived by the lies of these Jezebels or their father. Send them back where they came from – back to their Moorish lovers and their pagan prayers and their magic practices and their beds of red satin and lace! When my poor nephews found out the true nature of their *wives*, they cast aside all hope of wealth and advancement, and rode home in tears to my door, with a few miserable trinkets, rather than be tainted by the sins of these *loose women*. It is greatly to their honour! My family house gains honour by it. Would that they had struck harder with their spurs and kicked those she-devils all the way back to Hell from where they surely came!'

Sol gave a choked scream and fainted. Elvira trembled and swayed beneath her veil. Doña Jimena said, 'Señor Ordoñez. Your nephews have lied to you if they have told you this story. And you are lying to yourself if you believe them.'

El Cid, stepping still closer to the King, shouted, 'Justice! I look for justice! At the foot of the throne of Spain, I *demand* justice!'

'*Demand?*' Alfonso rose out of his throne. Courtiers dropped to their knees; the guard leapt to attention. 'You *demand* it, do you, señor? Look for it you may. Hope for it you might. But *demand* it? Never.' His lips, when he pursed them, turned bone white.

Count Ordoñez went and stood beside the throne, outfacing El Cid. 'You see, Sire? You see what airs he gives himself? You see how a few petty conquests have turned him into a king?' The room burst into uproar. Fernando and Diego came out from behind a tapestry and swaggered to their uncle's side.

Like a great tower, El Cid seemed suddenly under siege from all sides. Cries of 'Shame! Shame!' rained down as he knelt speechless beside little Sol. He did not hear the many voices that called out in his favour: 'Shame on the house of Carrión that it has spawned footpads and thieves!' 'Shame on you, Ordoñez, for defending them!'

Doña Jimena threw back her veil. They were silent then. Her pale face and huge eyes transfixed them all. 'Observe me, señors! Do you know me? I was the daughter of the Count of Seville when young Don Rodrigo Díaz came seeking my hand. My father – like the Count Ordoñez here – scorned his birth, defamed his family, though indeed he valued Rodrigo as the finest soldier in his troop. They fought. My father was killed.' Now even Sol was sitting up: this was a story she had never heard. 'For three days I tore my clothes and lay at the old King's feet and poured my hair into his lap along with my tears. "Rodrigo Díaz must pay for my father's life. Rodrigo Díaz must die! Rodrigo Díaz is a murderer!" But the King held firm. "In a fight over honour," he said, "God holds the sword of the victor." And when I looked into the face of the man who had killed my father, I knew that the King spoke the truth. Honour was on his sword. Now the names of Díaz and the Infantes hang soiled, and one must be washed clean with blood. My husband must fight the Infantes.'

Fernando put his hand over his brother's mouth to stifle the sound of his whimpering. 'Quiet. If we're quick and quiet, we can be out of León before the King has even made up his mind. Quick!'

The room was shocked into silence. Ordoñez whispered urgently in the King's ear, 'Think how it would dishonour the royal Infantes to fight a mere bastard peasant!'

Alfonso's lips moved, but he was speaking to himself. 'Two against one. Two against one,' he seemed to be saying. Then his face flinched as a trumpet blew at the door. He was not accustomed to being interrupted by trumpets.

With the draughty flutter of a falling tent, everyone in the room either curtsied or dropped to their knees. The Princes of Navarre and Aragón entered the room, without ceremony or grandeur. Dark and unadorned young men they were, with long curling hair, and half-cloaks worn over one shoulder.

'Forgive me, cousin,' said the young heir to Navarre. 'My brother and I have made so bold as to watch your proceedings from the minstrels' gallery. It would amuse us both to see the lady's challenge met.'

'But my lords! The dishonour!' cried the Count Ordoñez with venomous urgency. 'The Infantes would demean themselves to cross swords with this arrogant, illegitimate, upstart peasant!'

The Prince of Aragón smiled and bowed his head politely. 'As I hear tell, the King of Morocco himself thought it no dishonour to cross swords with this same upstart peasant. And surely Count Ordoñez, you will not deny us this entertainment.'

'No! No, he won't!' cried King Alfonso jumping to his feet. 'Prepare for a tournament! Prepare a grandstand! Let the Infantes put on armour . . . where are the Infantes? Where have they gone?'

'I believe you will find them in the stables, cousin,' said the Prince of Navarre helpfully. 'I happened to see them running inside, and I took the liberty of locking the doors on them.'

At either end of the lists, absurdly small tournament tents cracked like drums in the wind. The Infantes' shared tent bulged with sharp elbows and knees as the brothers, dressing for battle, broke off to fight with each other or broke off from fighting to put on one more piece of armour. Their arguing could be heard even at the far end of the lists:

'I wish I'd never listened to you!'

'It was your idea in the first place!'

'I'd never had done it if you hadn't kept on and on . . .'

'I should have drowned you the day you were born, little brother.'

Don Rodrigo had no need to change – he was already in armour, and mounted on Babieca. Alvar Fañez fussed round him, adjusting the hang of his sword, checking the buckle of the saddle. Babieca nipped at him irritably with her long, yellow teeth.

'Stand back, dear friend. The Infantes are mounting,' said El Cid.

'You will take care, won't you.'

'I will take care to be avenged,' said El Cid.

'I mean, there are two of them.'

'But they have half my grievances.'

'. . . and they are half your age!'

'Then I have twice their skill,' said El Cid.

'Oh, a thousand times their skill,' Fañez admitted with a nervous laugh as he remembered the battle with King Mu'taman and the incident with the lion. It comforted him to think of the incident with the lion.

As the combatants took up their lances, Sol and Elvira, seated beside their mother in the grandstand, put their hands inside their veils and covered their faces. Doña Jimena looked straight ahead.

'I regret the danger to your noble husband, madam,' said the Prince of Navarre.

'There is no danger, your Highness,' replied Doña Jimena, lifting her veil. 'God will protect the good, and I thank you for causing this fight to be fought.' There was a thunder of hooves, a clash of arms, a grunt. A horse neighed. The crowd gasped. The hoof beats picked up their frantic rhythm again. But the face of Doña Jimena did not flinch.

Suddenly the whole field of tournament seemed to be filled with horses. From behind the Infantes' tent came half the family of Carrión and all the friends of Count Ordoñez.

Immediately the men from Valencia leapt to their horses: Alvar Fañez, Bishop Pedro, Don Bermúdez, Martin the Miller, and Muño Gustioz. The grandstand stood half empty. The little arena milled like a stockyard when the cows catch wind of their slaughter, with animals shouldering and barging, their eyes rolling, their tongues flapping beneath the bit.

Ordoñez drove his spurs into the calf of Don Bermúdez as they passed each other, and his sword cut through three layers of his leather shield. Bermúdez drove his heels hard down in his stirrups and his horse, drawing in its head, leapt backwards, swinging its flanks against horse and rider. The girth of Ordoñez' saddle broke and he pitched on his head over his mare's rump.

Diego, in fleeing the sword of Bishop Pedro around the perimeter fence, found himself coming up hard on Alvar Fañez from behind. He shut his eyes, levelled his lance, and drove it at the unprotected back. At the last moment, Fañez turned and the lance tip split the layers of his shield, and tore through the chain mail of his sleeve. He laid both hands on Diego's lance and tore it out of his hands, bringing it up under the Infante's chin so that his teeth clashed shut and his eyes rolled. His hands, groping for balance, found Alvar Fañez' throat, and together they tumbled to the ground, where their swords bent beneath them. Diego was first to his feet – off and running for the gantry of seats where the King sat. Fañez brought him down with a dive at his heels, and he sprawled, winded, at Alfonso's feet, his fingers scrabbling for the King's ankles. '*Protection!*' he wheezed, trying to fix Alfonso's eyes with his own.

The King turned away his head.

Alvar Fañez got to his feet, drew his sword and, raising it in two hands, point downwards above Diego's face, drove it . . . into the ground.

The blade passed between the Infante's jaw and collarbone, and the vibrating metal grazed the beard off the plump underside of his chin. 'Go home to your ancestral halls, you great angora rabbit, and may fortune send you no children to help you carry your shame.' Sparks flew from his scabbard as Alvar Fañez sheathed the great sword Tizan.

Bishop Pedro and the Count Ordoñez clashed in the centre of the lists, and the central barrier was smashed between the horses' heaving flanks. The saddlecloth was pulled from under the Bishop's saddle and billowed out behind him as his horse sprang aside from the Count's whirling mace. Ordoñez let the mace fall and drew out his sword, hacking at the Bishop's horse and succeeding in cutting through the reins. Off went the horse around the arena, afraid and unrestrained. The Count followed after, sword raised to bring it down on the Bishop's back. One blow grazed away a layer of material.

But as Pedro passed the Infantes' tent, he pulled up a lance from the thicket of lances jammed into the soil there. And turning in the saddle, he swung the lance like a quarter-stave and struck Ordoñez clean out of the saddle to sprawl unconscious in the dust.

Babieca's big hooves lifted high to avoid stepping on the Count. She had no sooner collected herself than Don Rodrigo set her at the central barrier and they leapt it in pursuit of the Infante Fernando. Round and round the arena El Cid pursued Fernando, and the only blows the Infante threw were curses cast over his shoulder. Then, suddenly, at the foot of the lists, he turned his horse.

He was holding a short-sword, and he drove it at Rodrigo's face. It cut through the strap of his helmet, which bowled away between the confusion of horses' hooves and exposed El Cid's white linen coif. Rodrigo took hold of the Infante's sword hand and forced it open, finger by finger, until the short-sword dropped with a thud to the ground. Fernando could see his own reflection in the cold blue eyes. He heard the great sword Colada slide from its sheath, and his heart shrank like a pig from the butcher's blade. He turned his horse, but El Cid had hold of the horse's tail: he knotted his arm in it once and twice. The sword was out. The blade was falling. 'Please!' was all Fernando could say. '*Please!*'

'That's for the shame of my daughters; that for the betrayal of my trust; and that for calling me a bastard!' The blade slapped flat on Fernando's back. It shredded his clothing; even his chain mail fell into holes, but the cutting edge was turned aside. 'Now get back to school, *boy*, and learn yourself some manners!' At last El Cid released the horse and set it galloping with a smack to the rump.

It scattered all that was left of the Ordoñez horsemen. The lists were

empty. Don Rodrigo cut down the Infantes' tent, and it fell to the ground like a great sail emptying. 'To Valencia! Before the Moors!' he shouted, and there was a rattle of carts and bridles by way of an answer. The Infantes' treasure started on its way down the sun-bleached track, back to where it came from.

'A moment!' exclaimed the King, gathering up the skirts of his robe to hurry down from the grandstand. 'El Cid, the justice of your cause is proven – as We knew it would be from the very start! You have done León a great service today in exposing the rats in its cellars. Ordoñez and his nephews shall be driven out of the country today. Sooner! Come! Let Us embrace the noblest son of Castile! My admiration for El Cid is without end!'

Don Rodrigo dismounted. He was still breathing heavily after the fight. Alfonso too took a deep breath, then flung his arms round the man. He only flinched a little, as the silver cuirass dug into his chest. Rodrigo's beard enveloped the King's face: he had always stood that much taller than Alfonso.

The Princes of Navarre and Aragón stepped down too, each lending an arm to Doña Jimena. Just when everyone expected them to saunter away with a twirl of the wrist and a fashionable yawn, they dropped abruptly to their knees in front of the victor – their royal knees in the mud of the lists.

'These young gentlemen have not been idle during your show-of-arms,' said Doña Jimena. 'They have been casting their eyes over your noble daughters.'

'And though their veils were down, sir, we saw there a beauty of spirit past admiration,' said Navarre.

'They are like the tree struck by lightning which grows more green the next spring,' said Aragón.

'The Princes wish to marry our daughters, husband, and make them queens in the course of time.'

Don Rodrigo shook his head, and the faces of the Princes dropped so comically that he laughed for the first time in many months. 'Stand up, your royal highnesses. You honour me beyond my merit. But this time neither father nor King shall decide the fate of Sol and Elvira. This time they must decide for themselves whether they will have you or not. A man may lay siege to the fortress of a woman's heart, but only she may open its gates to let him in.'

Then he embraced the Princes, man to man, and walked away to his tourney tent hand-in-hand with Doña Jimena of Seville.

Murder at the Wedding

Don Rodrigo had meant to leave at once for Valencia. But the wedding of his daughters to the Princes of Aragón and Navarre at León Cathedral delayed him another whole day. There was bread to be broken at their marriage feast, and wine to be drunk to their good fortune.

A hard-rimmed moon rose out of the wheat fields, and the great dark mass of the palace looked like an irregular hole cut in the sky. The torches flickering along its highest fortifications mingled with the stars. The moonlight made silhouettes out of the dancers in the great tents on the lawn. One of the silhouettes was the tall, narrow-waisted figure of Rodrigo, his outline instantly recognizable by the shaggy poll of hair and that beard of great renown. He stood aloof from the dancing. He drank only sips of wine. His thoughts were in Valencia, watching and waiting for the revenge of the Moors.

Outside in the dark shadows, the Count Ordoñez was kept aloof from the dancing, prevented from drinking the wine. His family crest was shattered; his banners were in shreds; his name was dirtied past washing; and his possessions were all forfeit to El Cid. All that remained to him was shame and infamy. His friends shunned him; his servants shut in his face the doors of his own house. And Rodrigo the Bastard had not even honoured him with the sharp edge of his sword. For a knight, there is no defeat so crushing as mercy, no insult to match the shame of being spared.

The worms in the earth beneath his hands and knees were no more quiet in their creeping than the Count Ordoñez. In his fist was a knife, the blade blackened with tar so as not to catch the moonlight. It blackened his hands as he stood up and raised it in both fists – a grip like a man praying. The cloth of the tent was stretched a little round the shoulders and hips of the man inside. There was no hardness of armour, no mottling of chain mail. There was nothing but a shirt to protect the Conqueror's back.

The jewels were gone from Ordoñez' fingers. The knife blade was black. As he struck, nothing flashed but the rims of his eyes. He snatched his hands away quickly: through the tent, his fingers had touched the warm, flinching movement of the man's body.

'Is it done?' said the rider among the trees, holding out to Ordoñez the reins of a fast horse.

'A cowardly thing, to stab a man in the back,' replied Ordoñez in a small, broken voice.

'*Is it done, siddi?*'

'It is done.'

There was a flash of white teeth out of the darkness of a Moorish face. 'This is good. This is as Allah wills it. The thief of Valencia is killed, and the dishonour is on the hands of a cowardly Christian dog.'

'Father? Are you all right, Father?' Sol broke free from the dancing and ran towards him.

He was standing, as he had been, his shoulders against the tent's cloth, very upright and aloof. But the hand holding his wine goblet hung down by his side and the wine dribbled out on to the grass. His face was deathly white. 'Yes, yes,' he said, 'but may I crave your assistance, madam. To draw out my sword, if you please.' He was attempting to pull Colada out of its scabbard, using only his left hand. Sol quickly drew it out and offered him the hilt. 'No. My left hand, girl. Put it into my left.'

The music faltered. The dancing stopped. A hundred faces, moonish with flickering torchlight, turned towards El Cid. His hand closed round the hilt of the great sword; he turned; he drove the sword through the skin of the tent behind him. Like a drumskin it tore. Like a drumskin there was nothing but darkness and air beyond.

For a moment, the wedding guests thought Don Rodrigo had surprised an interloper. 'A spy! El Cid has killed a spy!' For there was blood on the canvas. But then they saw the short knife sticking in his back, and the torn tent canvas flapping. The night air seeped in through the tent, cold, cold, like water into a holed and sinking ship.

'Fetch a litter for my husband,' said Doña Jimena through the chaos of whispering. 'Fetch a litter and a surgeon!'

They did find the Count Ordoñez. He lay in among the nearby trees. His throat had been cut with a clean, Moorish knife.

'It's nothing,' said the King's surgeon. 'It's nothing but a scratch.' He was a man with a face hugely wrinkled, as though he had spent too long in this noxious atmosphere of his, this steaming mixture of smells, sweat, liniment and burning incense. He packed away his bone-handled tools neatly into their casket, and stood admiring them for a moment. His smile signified nothing, since he always wore it. He was inclined to giggle out of nervousness. 'A week's rest. An infusion of cayenne pepper. I understand the King himself is saying mass for you at this very moment. You must indeed be a great man, señor.'

'I must leave for Valencia at once. The Moors will be mustering. They've probably set sail already,' said Don Rodrigo feverishly.

Doña Jimena put her handkerchief to her mouth. 'That's impossible, my love. The good doctor says you must rest. Tell him, doctor. Tell him, he mustn't travel.'

The surgeon giggled. 'Well, I can't see . . . a little journey . . . if it's important . . .'

'Doctor! Do you know where Valencia is?' exclaimed Doña Jimena.

But his smile held fast, '. . . a little journey . . . if it's really necessary . . . I don't see what harm . . .' And he scuttered out of the room clutching his little casket of instruments.

'I thought the wound was deep! I don't understand!' Jimena called after him helplessly.

'I do,' said Don Rodrigo, and the dismal northern rain splashed in over the windowsill into his face.

At the foot of the stairs, the surgeon met King Alfonso returning from the Royal Chapel. 'Well? And have Our prayers been answered?'

The doctor giggled nervously. His grin never wavered. 'The outcome is always God's will, your Majesty. The knife blade wasn't clean. The wound was deep. He talks of going back to Valencia. A man should be buried in the place of his choice, I always think.'

King Alfonso gave a snort of impatience. 'You should not have let Us waste Our time in chapel, then. We are a busy man, you know.'

With agonizing slowness, the train of El Cid travelled south. Mattresses were piled four deep in his litter. The pot holes were filled, and rocks were cleared out of its path. Night and day his officers took turns to ride

alongside him, exchanging words with him. After crossing out of Castile, he refused to sleep at all.

'Go on ahead, Don Alvar Fañez. Lay in siege provisions. Forewarn the garrison that Mu'taman will be coming.'

'Surely it is important that they should hear it from your own lips, Commander, and see for themselves the unimportance of your wound. Let me stay with you.'

'Go on ahead, Alvar. The news of my injury has certainly reached Morocco already. Better they should worry a little in Valencia than be surprised in their beds by King Mu'taman.'

He was right. As the wind shakes sand from the robes of a bedouin, so the summons of King Mu'taman shook Moorish soldiers from every fold of his desert kingdom. Valencia must be recaptured, and nothing stood in the way now of a Moorish army of conquest.

The news of El Siddi's assassination almost saddened the King: he had sworn to meet the man once more on the battlefield and teach him the will of Allah. But he rewarded the spy who brought the news, for the thing was well done, and no dishonour stained Moroccan hands. He made no secret of setting sail, for he knew that the fear struck into the garrison at Valencia by the thought of his coming would be sharper than any sword.

Then news followed that El Siddi was not yet dead. King Mu'taman filled the sails of his ships with shouting: 'Raise more canvas, men! The wind is with us. Let not the Infidel Thief called Siddi make his deathbed inside the city of Allah!'

It was then that the wind dropped, and the sails emptied, and the Moors groaned and leaned on their oars. 'The ways of Allah are strange,' said the King, scowling at the sky.'

Slow and cautious at the start, the cavalcade moved faster and faster and faster, the closer it came to Valencia. A cloud like the Angel of Death stood in the northern sky, and the sun urged them to hurry south, with white hot beams which curled the long leaves into beckoning fingers.

Alvar Fañez came out of the city at the gallop to greet them. 'There are three thousand sails in the bay! The Moors are almost landed!' And the carriage piled high with mattresses rolled forward faster still, until the sweating horses broke into a gallop and the wheels jarred and the frame shook, and Babieca stretched out her neck to keep pace behind.

The walls of the city rushed forward to greet them; the minarets seemed to lean over and gaze down at the curtained wagon as it hurtled recklessly through the dark gates. There was not a man there but he put

one hand on his chest, feeling the knife wound jar as the wheels of the Conqueror's wagon struck the cobbled streets.

The moon laid a sickening pallor on the houses. The stars pricked like pain. The cloud shaped like the Angel of Death had disappeared, for now the whole sky was black.

But Valencia blazed with light to welcome home its saviour. Along the streets, every soul of the city cheered and clamoured to celebrate the homecoming of El Cid. They reached out to touch the curtained wagon as it creaked past, then danced home and slept well, feeling safe, for all there were three thousand sails in the bay. 'El Cid will save us from the Moors,' they said.

At the steps of the palace, six men took hold of the topmost mattress and carried El Cid indoors. They ran with him, up the steps, across the marble floors that rang with joy at the sound of their feet; beneath the ceilings carved with Arabic prayers; between the pillars twisted like the hair of an anxious woman. Servants crouched beneath the oak stairs whispered, 'El Cid has come home to save us from the Moors.'

Alvar Fañez was one of the six, and as they ran, he explained breathlessly to his commander what preparations he had made for a siege: 'In terms of food, we can hold out for a month without hardship. The well water is secure. I sank seventeen merchant ships in the harbour mouth to block it. I've sent to Barcelona for help. When you're recovered, we'll make a sortie to drive off the Moors. Don't worry about a thing. Valencia can wait for your recovery. Getting strong again – that's all you need think of now.'

They laid the mattress down on top of the white bed of the ousted Siddi, and went down on their knees to show respect. No one dared look his commander in the face for fear of seeing him suffer.

Don Alvar began to repeat what he had said about preparing for the siege, but Doña Jimena touched him on the shoulder and said, 'You have done well, Don Alvar. You have done all you could. Go now and rest. I promise you that my husband has no worries on any matter. But I beg you, gentlemen, to say a prayer for him before you sleep tonight.'

'Yes, yes! A prayer for his speedy recovery!' said Fañez eagerly.

'No, no, gentlemen. A prayer for his soul.' She went to the bedside and drew back the blanket from the Conqueror's face. His linen coif was crumpled as if he had just pushed back a chain-mail hood, and his greying hair and beard spilled out round its rim as the cotton boll spills in ripening. Doña Jimena put the fingers of one hand on his cheek. She lifted her veil better to see his face. 'El Cid has returned to Valencia, gentlemen, but my sweet husband is in a better place still. With the angels he lays siege to the throne of God. Don Rodrigo Díaz de Vivar has been dead this past hour.'

Rider to the World's End

'Our commander is dead?'

'The Don of Vivar dead!'

'The Conqueror dead!'

'El Cid is dead!'

A wail went through the city that curdled the blood in the red-veined stones, that silenced the chattering fountains, that sent a shiver up the spiral columns of the tall minarets. 'El Cid is dead!'

Great black banners were draped over the city wall, and black flags flapped against the night sky, invisible as the wings of the Angel of Death. And the cathedral bell of Saint Estabán clanged,

'*El Cid is dead.*

El Cid is dead.'

By dawn, fifty thousand Moors were camped beneath the orange trees. They rose early to see the beautiful city of Allah laid bare by the retreating darkness. At the sight of the black banners, a dull subhuman murmur swelled and grew into a roar, a universal cheer. The Moors danced barefoot in the dew, and beat with hooked drumsticks on the bruised skins of drums, and chanted, 'El Siddi is dead! El Siddi is dead!'

Spies and terrified turncoats darted out from under the skirts of the city wall and confirmed their best hopes – that El Siddi was dead, El Siddi had died.

Doña Jimena watched them dance from her window. In the face of their frenzied dashing to and fro, Valencia felt as fragile as a sandcastle scoured round by the sea: one push and it would fall flat, and El Cid's men and women would be washed away in a tide of blood. 'I thank God that our daughters are safe and happy,' she said aloud, although of course no answer came from the bed. 'We are lost without you, my dear. You leave us in the very jaws of the lion. Nothing can save us now.'

A breeze lifted the tapestry on the wall. Its hem brushed the table. A bundle on the table rolled off it, and Don Rodrigo's chain mail spilled out on the floor. Jimena gave a little startled cry. 'Oh! Must I suffer even that? Must I lose even what I have?'

After a moment, though, she called the doorkeeper and said, 'Ask Bishop Pedro to come to me in a little while.' Then she gathered up the chain mail in her arms.

Bishop Pedro came, in surplice and cope, with a little African altar boy swinging incense on a chain. His mind was full of funerals and words of comfort. Opening the chamber door, the altar boy shrieked, threw down the censer and fled, pushing the Bishop aside. Pedro called after him, then turned back into the room . . . and was confronted by the sight of El Cid seated in a chair in full battle dress.

Crouched under one arm was his wife, dishevelled and sweating, her long hair jumbled and tumbling to the floor. 'He's too heavy for me,' she panted.

The Bishop dropped his psalter and ran to shoulder the weight, pulling Rodrigo's other arm across his back without knowing why. 'Lady! What madness is this? Do you think to bring him back to life by force? What are you thinking of? Has grief taken your wits?'

'No time for grieving, sir,' she gasped, screwing up her face with the effort of lifting. 'I have the rest of my life for that. Help me carry him down the back stairs. The fewer who see us the better.'

It was very like a nightmare, carrying the cold dead weight down the spiral stairs, the toes of Rodrigo's boots scuffing and bumping down each stone step. There was a winch above the rear door or they could never have got Rodrigo on to his horse. Babieca's eyes rolled, and she ground the bit between her teeth and flared her nostrils at the changed sight and smell of her rider. The feet in her stirrups were stiff; the thighs in her saddle were rigid.

They needed no board for his back: in death the upright spine kept its proud, erect bearing. The base of his lance they wedged into one stirrup, and they bound his hand high up on the lance-grip so that his right arm was at full stretch. They passed a rope through beneath the horse, to link the feet. They bound his calves to the saddle. They ran ties from his belt to both crupper and pommel. There was no way of preventing his head from lolling forwards on to his chest, but the great volume of his beard supported his chin a little. They stood back, sweating and utterly exhausted.

'Open his eyes,' said Doña Jimena coldly.

'Lady! For pity's sake! It's the last service a man requires – that those who love him should close his eyes in death! Will you have your husband ride into eternity with his eyelids up?'

'Open his eyes,' said Jimena. Her face was whiter than the rider's.

The city began to stir. Subdued and despairing, the people rose from their beds before dawn, as if there was too little time left to waste on sleep. One by one, the officers of El Cid attended on his widow to offer what comfort they could. They gathered in the great hall of the palace.

'Shall we make a sortie, then?' said Don Bermúdez wearily.

'Better to throw ourselves on the Moors' swords than to starve to death after a year or two,' said Alvar Fañez.

'Much better to enter Heaven close behind El Cid,' said Martin the Miller.

'First I shall pay my respects to Doña Jimena and to the Conqueror's body, then I shall throw myself on the Moors and die fighting in the name of Valencia and El Cid,' said Muño Gustioz, and he stamped angrily up the stairs. A moment later he came tumbling down them again: 'He's gone! He's not there! His armour's gone! His wife's gone!'

They ran, without knowing where they were running, out of the palace. They mounted their horses and rode frantically to and fro, converging at last on the front gates of the city. Alvar Fañez could not keep himself from calling out: 'Commander! Don Rodrigo, sir! El Cid! Where are you?' So that grilles were thrown back and doors opened, and the city was roused.

When the riders caught sight of Doña Jimena and the Bishop and the

mounted figure and the upraised right hand on the lance, each man experienced a momentary surge of hope, a fleeting belief in miracles. They threw aside common sense and fear. They stopped believing in death and they threw their horses towards the city gates as if these were the Gates of Heaven itself.

The huge main gates were bolted shut. The small side gate was open. Babieca's wide flanks almost touched either side of its narrow arch. The golden mail of El Cid's hood grazed the keystone. At the noise of galloping horses behind her, Babieca started forward and was through the gate. El Cid's officers hurled through behind her, bending low in their saddles, ducking the arch. Babieca felt the urgency of battle and, stretching out her neck, led the wild and desperate charge. The first the Moors knew was that the foray was in among them, galloping out of a rising sun.

They sprang from their tents to see riders coming, in silhouette. The bright beams half closed the irises of their dark eyes. They saw the lead rider – a lance bearer with a massive sword by his side. They saw the colourless sheen of his chain mail gleaming like a snake's skin. They saw escaping wisps of hair lit like the sun's corona round the head. They saw, as the rider closed on them, pasty features gaunt as a skull, teeth clenched, and the blue eyes wildly staring, the white knuckles of the hand upraised on the lance.

'El Siddi!' The thought stuck in their throats and choked them.

'El Siddi!' The sight curdled their blood.

'El Siddi!' Babieca's hooves crushed their bare feet as they stood paralysed with fear. 'El Siddi lives!' Babieca barged them on to their faces. 'No! El Siddi's *spirit* lives!'

They were spoken, those words of blackest magic, that unthinkable dread, that horror Allah himself could not forbid. And at once the words were in every mind. '*El Siddi's spirit lives!*'

When Babieca spilled them to the ground, they did not drag themselves clear or draw their swords or tuck in their knees. The Christian officers following reaped them like nettles, harrowed them like clods. And though, one by one, they were cut down – Fañez and Bermúdez, Martin and Gustioz – by scimitar or spear, arrows or daggers, no Moor dared even to look in the face of the lead rider. All they did was to cover their faces with their cloaks and wail, 'El Siddi's spirit has come for us!'

Then the hindermost men began to run. They threw down their curved swords. They fumbled with the hobbles on their horses, they left their headgear in the trees. They rode towards the sea, and did not stop when they got there. They rode straight in, with huge splashes of spray, their horses screaming with alarm. Some were cut down by their

commanders, but that did not stop the mutiny. The mutineers had no fear of human violence – not when behind them came a spirit with the power to slay their souls. 'Don't you see?' they howled at their officers. 'El Siddi's spirit has come for us! He will slay us through all eternity!' And then the Moorish commanders fled too.

King Mu'taman, loose robed and barefoot, lay in his tent – a tent embroidered from hem to crown with Arabic cyphers: '*Glory to Allah, the only true God.*' In the pale morning light, the shadows of the embroidery fell on him like the shadows of lizards and locusts crawling overhead. The King shivered without knowing why. Then he heard the shouting. He siezed his sword and sprang into the open, calling for his horse. He saw the rider, saw the upraised hand, the undrawn sword, the staring blue eyes – for he was standing directly in Babieca's path.

'Allah is God of the living and the dead. You are no spirit!' he mouthed at the pale, clenched features, and lifting his sword over his shoulder like a javelin, he hurled it, point-first, at the heart of El Cid. It penetrated the chest, for there was no cuirass. It penetrated flesh and rib and the cold, sleeping heart, and it came out through his back. Rodrigo neither slowed his horse nor swayed in the saddle, nor gave one blink of his wild, blue eyes, but rode on over the King. And the third sword that he captured in his heart rivalled in beauty the great swords called Tizan and Colada.

Mu'taman lay in the grass, beneath the prayer-covered flap of his tent, and murmured, 'I come, El Cid, to fight you through all eternity, to the everlasting glory of Allah.'

The sea boiled with swimmers. The ships anchored off shore sank under the burden of fugitives trying to clamber aboard. The stones of Valencia watched in pitiless silence, and the orange trees groaned in a rising wind.

Far beyond the turmoil of terror in the bay, a single horseman continued on his inexorable path. Hock-deep in sand, Babieca defied the fingers of surf that groped at her hooves. The sun rose further, scorching out all detail in a white haze of heat. Both horse and rider were lost in the wavering light, the hoof prints extinguished by the greedy sea.

And though Doña Jimena sent trusted men to search the far shore and inland woods, no trace was ever found of the man called El Cid. No grave cradled him, nor cupped flowers grew to catch the tears of those who mourned him.

Nor did the earth clog his features, nor Time smother his memory. For the glory of El Cid is without ending in the history of Spain.

Oxford University Press, Walton Street, Oxford OX2 6DP
Oxford New York Toronto
Delhi Bombay Calcutta Madras Karachi
Petaling Jaya Singapore Hong Kong Tokyo
Nairobi Dar es Salaam Cape Town
Melbourne Auckland

and associated companies in
Berlin Ibadan

Oxford is a trade mark of Oxford University Press

Text © James Riordan 1988
Illustrations © Victor G Ambrus 1988

Oxford University Press 1988
First published by Oxford USA 1989

British Library Cataloguing in Publication Data

Collodi, Carlo
Pinocchio.
Rn: Carlo Lorenzini   I. Title
II. Riordan, James   III. Ambrus, Victor
853.8[J]   PZ7
Library of Congress Catalog Card Number 89–42964
ISBN 0 19 279855 3

Typeset by PGT Graphic Design, Oxford
Printed by Singapore National Printers Ltd